Brainblocks

Brainblocks

Overcoming the
7 Hidden Barriers
to Success

THEO TSAOUSIDES, PHD

PRENTICE HALL PRESS

PRENTICE HALL PRESS
An imprint of Penguin Random House LLC
375 Hudson Street, New York, New York 10014

BRAINBLOCKS

ISBN: 978-0-7352-0545-1

This book has been registered with the Library of Congress.

First edition: August 2015

PRINTED IN THE UNITED STATES OF AMERICA

10 9 8 7 6 5 4 3 2 1

Text design by Kristin del Rosario

Most Prentice Hall Press books are available at special quantity discounts for bulk
purchases for sales promotions, premiums, fund-raising, or educational use.
Special books, or book excerpts, can also be created to fit specific needs.
For details, write: SpecialMarkets@penguinrandomhouse.com.

To my loving parents

CONTENTS

Do you ever wonder why some people accomplish so much in their lives and others keep falling short? What makes some people give up on their goals while others continue to persist? Why some people take forever to start working on their life goals and others need no second reminder?

This book is about you and your goals. It is about the seven main reasons why you haven't achieved your goals yet. It is about your *brainblocks*. Your habits of thinking, feeling, and acting that keep you stuck in place, get you off track, and make you move around in circles. You know what they are. You experience them daily. But what you may not know is what causes them. Only by knowing the reasons they exist will you be able to remove them. This book is a journey of discovering the secrets of success hiding inside your brain.

The New Year's Resolution Conundrum

How often do you come up with brilliant ideas about how to improve your life, how to boost your productivity, how to make more money, how to get a big promotion, how to be more fit and healthy, how to find love, how to help people fulfill their dreams, or simply how to just enjoy life more?

How often do you make promises that you will kick your bad habits and replace them with new ones that will put you on the express lane to success?

How often do you feel ready to make that important decision that will change your life forever?

If you are like most people, you do all that at least once a year! Along with counting down to zero and giving passionate kisses, making new resolutions is the most popular New Year's tradition. New beginnings, new promises, renewed passion, and high hopes for a better body, a better salary, or a better love life!

But . . . how often do you say: Yes! I did it! I hit the jackpot!

Again, if you are like most people, not often enough. As soon as the New Year's festivities are over, the resolutions become faint memories. The truth is that most of us fail to achieve the goals we set on New Year's. We forget, we get stalled, or we give up. Year after year we state the same goals, we make the same promises, and we repeat the same excuses, but we see no results.

Does failing to achieve our goals apply only to our New Year's resolutions? Or do all our goals have the same fate? Have we been sentenced to living a life without success?

A World Without Success Stories

Regardless of how you define it, success is something all people want. Success comes in many varieties. It can be small or big, daily or lifelong, material or spiritual, humble or grandiose, and noble or lowly. Regardless of its size, scope, or intention, success invariably starts with *setting* a goal and ends with *achieving* a goal. But the most important part of success is what lies between setting and achieving your goal. And that is *pursuing* a goal. That's what success is: deciding what you want (setting), working to make it happen (pursuing), and checking it off your list (achieving).

The simplest definition of *success*:

Setting, pursuing, and
achieving your goal

There is a plethora of resources and countless experts out there all intended to inspire and teach people how to set and achieve goals. There is something for everyone in the self-help buffet. Books, videos, podcasts, blogs, webinars, live events, trainings, and coaching on anything imaginable, from how to be rich or healthy to how to be cool or sexy. The self-help industry is like the Costco of good advice.

Despite the abundance of resources, the truth is that most people *talk* about things they want in life, but relatively few actually *set* goals, and even fewer *achieve* them. The proportion of people who successfully achieve their goals is similar across different settings: no more than 10 percent! For example, studies have shown that among all people who set New Year's resolutions, only 8 percent actually achieve them.[1] Two months after the beginning of the year, most of us barely remember *what* our resolution was!

The same 10 percent success rate is evident in the self-help industry. While this industry generates billions of dollars annually from products and services, statistics show a dismal 10 percent success rate in terms of people achieving their goals.

Imagine the impact on society if only 10 percent of physicians, teachers, urban planners, business owners, or judges were able to achieve their goals. What would this low level of success rate mean for the health, education, livelihood, sustenance, and legal rights of the millions of people they serve?

What if the goals you set for yourself had the same fate? What would your life be like if you could only achieve 10 percent of what you hoped for? What if nine out of ten things you wished to accomplish never happened? My guess is that a 90 percent failure rate of achieving personal, professional, financial, academic, humanitarian, or any other type of goal would very quickly make this world a very depressive, pessimistic, and bitter place to live in.

The Tough Part of Success

There are armies of experts on multiple topics offering hundreds of methods for *setting* and *achieving* goals, with promises that range from getting things done to making dreams come true.

I am one of those experts. My job is to help people set and achieve goals. For that reason, I have a big investment in their success. I teach them a broad range of skills and strategies they can use to achieve their goals. I make sure the techniques I choose are tested and proven. What I do is based on science, backed by research, and used in many contexts, including businesses, organizations, medical settings, and schools. I even use these techniques myself to achieve my own goals.

But the truth is that techniques alone don't work. Regardless of how effective we, the experts, claim them to be and despite the number of testimonials that we can provide to support the power of our methods, the reality is that a large number of people will continue to fail.

And they fail because the most important factor in any success equation is not the method but the person who uses it. The key to success is what you *do* with what you know. And what you *do* is entirely controlled by you, not by the experts.

I have worked with hundreds of people with a wide range of goals. Some wanted to be more successful at work. Others wanted to be better at making decisions or wanted to be more loved. And some just wanted to be happier. What has always been true is that some of them are able to accomplish their goals fast and others keep struggling. After many years of observing and learning, I made an important discovery. I realized what is different about the 10 percent of achievers. It isn't the methods. It isn't their genes, personalities, education, gender, or upbringing. It is a simple and observable characteristic: They *pursue*. They *work* toward what they want. Achievers take *action*.

Setting a goal is fun and inspiring. It raises your motivation, it gets your spirits high, and it gives you something to look forward to. Promising yourself that you will eat more nutritious foods or that you will look for a more rewarding job or that you will travel more is very stimulating. *Achieving* a goal is rewarding and exciting. Seeing the results of your labor gives you a sense of satisfaction and fulfillment. But while the experts will show you how to set goals and will keep you pumped by reminding you what it feels like to achieve your goal, no one will tell you much about the most effortful and mundane part of success: *pursuing* the goal.

Pursuing a goal refers to taking all the steps you need to take to turn your vision into reality. It refers to the little and big tasks you have to do on a daily basis in order to accomplish your goal. It is the way in which you turn an idea into a plan and a plan into action. It is tracking your progress and adjusting your course. Pursuing is taking action. And that's the part that the 90 percent of nonachievers flunk.

Action is the essential ingredient of success

Action is the essential ingredient of success. Whether your goal is to lose weight, write a book, build your dream home, or find love, the only way to get there is by doing something. Any goal you set requires action. And action starts and stops in the brain.

How the Biggest Asset Can Become the Biggest Setback

Our brains are wired for success. They are designed to set, pursue, and achieve goals. They all come equipped with a set of mechanisms that enable them to do that. These mechanisms are called cognitive functions, and they are involved in receiving, storing, transforming, and using information from our internal and our external environment. For example, attention is the cognitive function that focuses us on what information is relevant to our goals at any given moment. Should I be listening to the conversation between those two lovebirds sitting at the table next to me or should I stay focused on finishing this paragraph?

Achieving success involves several cognitive functions. Our ability to set intentions, to envision the outcomes, to plan and strategize, to assess risk, to initiate our efforts, to keep track of our progress, to overcome obstacles, and to eventually celebrate our successes are all a result of our cognitive functions. And while all brains come equipped with these functions, not everyone knows how they work or how to use them more efficiently. For example, you are all aware that you can remember things that you have learned in the past, and that the brain function responsible for storing that information is called *memory*. You also know that sometimes your memory fails and you end up forgetting things. Think about the last time you went grocery shopping. Do you remember which grocery store you went to? Or how many items you bought? What you were wearing? The name of the person at the register? How much you paid? What song was playing as you were checking out? How many of these questions can you answer with 100 percent certainty?

Here is a challenge for you. Next time you go to the grocery store, try to remember the name of the grocery store, the number of items you buy, what clothes you have on, the name of the person at the register, the exact amount of money you need to pay, and what song is playing as you check out. How many of these questions do you think you will be able to answer with 100 percent certainty this time? Clearly, you will remember more than before. What does that mean? That your memory function improved between visits to the grocery store? Doubtful. What it means is that you used your memory function—your brain's ability to store information—differently the second time. You were actively concentrating, you used memorization techniques, and what was unimportant and forgettable became important and memorable. As a result you were much more successful in retaining the information and answering the questions.

The same is true for all of the brain's cognitive functions. The more efficiently we use them, the better we are at accomplishing our goals. The less efficiently we use them, the lower our odds of success. Using your memory efficiently means learning and memorizing information in a way that helps you retain what you need to remember in the future, relevant to your goals. If your goal is to answer the grocery store questions listed earlier, you need to pay attention and memorize the answers. You could write them down, record them on your phone, or repeat them in your head until you know them by heart. If your goal is to get a good raise this year, you need to memorize the three salary negotiation techniques you learned at the recent seminar you attended called "How to Make Killer Negotiations" and remember to use them when you have that uncomfortable talk about the raise with your boss.

Brainblocks:
How Our Brains Undermine Our Success

Our cognitive functions are subject to glitches. These glitches block our ability to focus, to think creatively, and to make decisions, and as a result, they affect our actions and how we pursue our goals. They create confusion and congestion, and as a result, we stop doing and we start drifting, stalling, or retracting. Our actions become purposeless and ineffective and no longer serve our goals.

Such glitches happen a lot. So often, in fact, that after a while, they not only distort our actions but affect the types of goals we set, the kinds of outcomes we expect, and even the way we think about ourselves and others. We begin attributing successes to good fortune, good genes, or good habits and failures to bad luck, irreversible personality flaws, or poor habits.

What we need to recognize is that how we think and what we do starts and ends in the brain. Personality traits that we traditionally associate with stagnation, inefficiency, failure, and despondency are nothing more than brainblocks: the products of glitches and the consequences of inefficient use of our brains. Brainblocks are the habits of feeling, thinking, and doing created by our brains that block our pursuit of success. And only our brains, or how we use them, can undo them.

Brainblocks are the enemy of action. They turn motivation to inertia, productivity to busywork, and dreamers to languishers. They cause an array of problems, ranging from diminished productivity and strained relationships to serious clinical problems, like depression and anxiety. Slowly and systematically, they end up killing our dreams.

What are the seven brainblocks and how do they undermine your success? In the next few chapters you will learn exactly what they are, how they affect you, what causes them, and how to remove them. You will learn what causes the *self-doubt* that blocks you from taking action and the *procrastination* that delays you indefinitely from getting things done. You will learn why *impatience* makes you rush into action prematurely and how *multitasking*, despite all the good press it gets, can shatter your focus into a thousand little pieces. You will learn how *rigidity* renders you blind to opportunities and why *perfectionism* keeps you far from perfection. You will learn that *negativity* is the best way to put an end to your dreams. And most important, you will learn what to do to remove these brainblocks and clear your path to success.

Brain Management: Removing the Brainblocks

We have the equipment, we have the abilities; now let's put them to use and smash our brainblocks. Our brains are powerful, and knowing how to manage them better will resolve a wide range of problems.

Brain management is the ability to use our cognitive functions in the best possible way and prevent the brain glitches from becoming brainblocks. Brain management is essential for success because it aligns our actions with our goals.

Brain management is made up of two parts: *awareness* and *engagement*. Awareness means *knowing* what the brainblocks are, what causes them, how they interfere with goal pursuit, and how to defeat them. Engagement means *doing* what you now know is necessary to develop new ways of thinking and acting and be able to achieve any goal you set.

Awareness and engagement work synergistically. One cannot happen without the other. To get something done, you need to know what to do. And simply knowing what to do alone does not mean you will do it. Brain management is about turning knowledge into action. Knowing the brain's tricks allows you to actually *do* something differently. For example, if you know that you tend to procrastinate, you also know that you should start working on a project much sooner, to avoid missing a deadline. But do you think that just because you *know* that, you will actually start *working* on the project sooner? Procrastinators do not suffer from lack of awareness. They suffer from lack of engagement.

Given how fast the brain learns, brain management can quickly change the way you approach your goals, your work, and your entire life. However, here is an important disclaimer: Even with good brain management, the brainblocks themselves can never be fully eliminated because they are generated by brain mechanisms with tremendous evolutionary value. They exist to protect you and to guarantee your survival. This is why the solution is *management* and not once-and-for-all elimination. Management is about monitoring, adjustment, and progress. You may feel insecure from time to time, you may put things off till the last minute for many "last minutes," and you may keep whining about your bad luck, even though you promised to never complain again. Such slips are normal. Managing your brainblocks means catching yourself in the act to prevent them from becoming success blocks. Eliminating the brainblocks, on the other hand, is unrealistic and impractical.

How to Use This Book

Brainblocks is a guide to removing the blocks and restoring action. To do that successfully, first you need to learn to recognize the characteristic feelings, thoughts, and actions associated with each brainblock. When you are able to recognize the brainblocks and how they affect your daily life, you will be able to remove them more easily. You will learn strategies to undo the glitches that cause them and to create new habits that promote action. The techniques you will learn make *awareness* easy and *engagement* even easier. By managing your brainblocks, you will be able to remove the obstacles that stand between setting and achieving a goal, the obstacles that stand between you and your dreams.

Each chapter is dedicated to one brainblock. The order of the chapters is not random. They are sequenced in a way that reflects the order in which the brainblocks interfere with your goal pursuit from start to finish. Some brainblocks won't let you get started, and others won't let you finish.

Even if you don't read the chapters in sequence but choose to focus on the brainblock that you see as the biggest obstacle in your life, I recommend reading all the chapters because you may be surprised by how many of the things you say or do have serious side effects on your goals without your even realizing it!

Each chapter is divided into five sections:

- **THE CONFESSIONAL.** In this section, I share my own and other people's stories and examples, to show what happens when the brainblock is activated. You will learn about the secret ways in which we sabotage ourselves, without even noticing.
- **SPOTTING THE BRAINBLOCK.** In this section, you will find an in-depth description of the brainblock in question, including the characteristic thoughts, feelings, and actions that it creates, so you can recognize it more easily in your own daily life.
- **BEHIND THE BRAINBLOCK.** In this section, you will learn what types of glitches or misuses in brain functioning cause the brainblock and how brain science and psychology explain the symptoms.
- **BRAINBLOCK SIDE EFFECTS.** Brainblocks can have serious consequences for your physical, mental, emotional, and spiritual health. In this section, you will find out what happens when you fall victim to your own brainblocks and what the future has in store for you, if you don't manage them.
- **SMASHING THE BRAINBLOCK.** In this section, you will be shown action strategies designed to train your brain to manage the brainblock, so you can remove it from your path to success and prevent it from becoming a permanent obstacle.

As you read through the book, try to be more mindful. Observe your own thoughts, feelings, and actions. What do you tell yourself when you start thinking about your goals? How do you carry out tasks during the day? How do you interact with other people? Are your actions helping you move forward or are they signs and symptoms of your brainblocks?

Focus on the strategies. Decide which ones work better for you and start applying them. Practice them. Remind yourself that to accomplish anything, you need to take action. And action is the key to removing the brainblocks from your path to success.

Before You Begin

Before you read further, take a minute and think about your most desired goal, something that you have been yearning after for a long time but haven't yet been able to accomplish. Maybe a stress-free life or a job that you actually love. A talent that you would like to develop, a trip that you have always wanted to take, a canvas waiting for you to paint on, or a parent who is hoping for forgiveness for ugly words uttered in the past.

What is the reason these goals have not become reality yet? Which brainblocks get in your way?

Enjoy this journey of discovery and make this the last year you have to set the same New Year's resolution!

SELF-DOUBT

Facing the Monster Within

Self-doubt is the brainblock with many names. We call it lack of confidence, insecurity, self-consciousness, shyness, low self-esteem, no faith in oneself, and so on. A rose by any other name would smell as sweet or, in this case, as pungent. Self-doubt is not a rose. It is a fundamental lack of trust in yourself. It is a lack of conviction in your potential to achieve a goal. It is the flipside of confidence. It is fear.

Self-doubt is the most fundamental brainblock, because it stops you from getting started. Not knowing what to do is scary. Fear chokes action and makes you feel vulnerable. You start to question your own abilities, your smarts, your strength, and your potential for success. Your focus shifts from what to do to how to protect yourself. Eventually, you get stalled.

Self-doubt dictates what you can and cannot do in

life. It determines how big your goals are, how high you set the bar, how far you want to reach. It keeps your ambition fenced. It supplies your mind with messages about how little you know, how undeveloped your skills are, how unfit for success you are, how difficult it is to make your dreams come true, how uncomfortable and overwhelmed you feel.

Self-doubt is not the same as healthy awareness of your weaknesses. Knowing your strengths and weaknesses is a key component of success. By spotting your weaknesses you find ways to work around them. By doubting your ability, however, you abandon your efforts. Healthy awareness leads to action. Self-doubt leads to inaction. It makes your weaknesses appear enormous and your goals unreachable. It forces you to deprioritize your goals, to put them on the back burner, and to make them secondary.

The Confessional

Peter is vice president of sales for an international luxury brand. He worked very hard to get to that position. He started out as part-time floor salesperson for a multinational clothing company's local store, but fairly quickly he became a lot more than that. A year after he started, he was promoted to assistant manager and after two more years to store manager. Because he was doing so well, he was moved to a more central location and became manager of one of the busiest stores in the downtown area of a big metropolis. Within a year, his store became one of the most profitable in the company's long list of retail shops. The next move was inevitable. Peter was promoted to regional manager, overseeing more than twenty stores. He climbed up the management ladder at unprecedented speed. He was one of those born-to-be-a-manager people. Peter didn't come from a family of CEOs, he didn't have an MBA, and in fact, he didn't even have a bachelor's degree. But he was focused, ambitious, and a hard worker.

But with promotions come responsibilities. And one of those responsibilities included participating in upper management meetings, where managers, directors, vice presidents, and CEOs all gather to review, report, and plan the company's future. Each regional manager was expected to give a presentation to the quorum, a brief overview of how the store was doing. This was Peter's first such meeting, and he was very apprehensive. He had no experience with public speaking. When it was his turn to go up, his knees started giving out. He barely made it to the podium. He uttered a couple of incomprehensible sentences, and then silence. He kept looking down and could not articulate a single word. Fraught with embarrassment, he decided that the best thing to do was to go back to his seat, and skip the presentation, leaving the audience puzzled and equally speechless.

Days went by. Peter hadn't heard from his bosses, who maybe out of compassion, confusion, or annoyance didn't say anything about the event. But he was having his own self-punishment meetings in his head. He kept hearing a voice, a derisive hiss, repeating in a stern tone:

"You can't do the job." Peter was brainblocked. Doubts started filling every curve and corner in his brain. The doubts went beyond fear of public speaking. He started questioning his abilities, his potential for more promotions, and his career choices. The self-doubt was so overwhelming that it started interfering with his work, affecting his relationships, and making his life miserable. Two months later, he resigned, leaving behind him what could be a very successful career. He spent the next twelve months unemployed, uninspired, and scared about his future.

That's self-doubt.

Spotting the Brainblock

Each brainblock has a characteristic action. The primary action of self-doubt is *hesitating*. You are always on the brink of taking action, but you don't take the next step. You are standing at the edge of the diving board contemplating whether you should jump, but you don't. You stop pursuing.

Primary Action:

You hesitate

What are the signs of self-doubt?

1. YOU BELIEVE THAT . . .

Your problems are bigger than your ability to solve them
You don't think you have the skills, the talent, the personality, or the energy to deal with challenges.

You have nothing to offer
What you have to say is not valuable, you can't have a meaningful impact on someone's life, you can't make an important contribution to the world, and no one gives two hoots about your message.

You are doing the best you can
You don't take on bigger bites than you can chew, you don't want to choke. You know that many things in life are out of your reach, so you mitigate your expectations of success accordingly.

You have to agree when you want to disagree . . .
Even if you think you are right, you'd rather be perceived as nice and agreeable than confrontational and argumentative.

. . . especially at work
You won't approach your boss for a promotion or a raise. You don't point out problems. You follow all the rules and procedures. You appear to have no initiative, no confidence, no aspiration.

2. YOU AVOID . . .

Trying new things
New people, new environments, and new activities seem
like chores.

Social situations
You don't start conversation easily, you speak softly if at
all, you avoid eye contact, stare at the floor, and stand in
corners, behind pillars, or near the exit. Your favorite
moment is when you leave.

The spotlight
It blinds you. Being the center of attention makes you
uncomfortable. You will not take the stage, you will
not make the toast, and you will not volunteer to sing
karaoke.

Feedback
You are vulnerable to criticism. You don't share opinions,
you don't share ideas, you don't share creations, to avoid
being criticized. Even if you think that your creations are
fabulous, when it's time to show the world, you would
rather hide them in the closet.

And also big life changes
You are very sluggish at achieving goals like quitting a
job you don't like, pursuing a new career path, going back
to school to study something you like, moving to a new
town, buying a house, breaking up, getting married, having children.

3. YOU CRAVE . . .

Security
You'd rather stay in your comfort zone: the comfort of your own home, the company of close family and friends, and the ease of your familiar routines.

And reassurance
On the one hand, you avoid feedback; on the other, you need encouragement. You need to be told that you are doing the right thing and that it's OK to keep going. So you ask for feedback from the people that you know will support you no matter what.

4. YOU ARE AFRAID . . .

To stand up for yourself
Defending yourself and backing your opinion is hard.

Especially around bullies
You are uncomfortable around people who come across as ultra-assertive and confident. When they actually become aggressive you feel intimidated and want to retreat into to your own shell even more.

Who make you doubt
And second-guess yourself a lot.

Behind the Brainblock:
Failure to Suppress Fear

THE BRAIN'S BODYGUARD

One of the most important tasks assigned to your brain is to protect you from danger and keep you safe. When your brain registers threat, it activates the sympathetic nervous system, the part of your nervous system that controls the body's *acute stress response*, which you probably know by its more popular name: fight-or-flight response. The fight-or-flight response is an ancient neurological mechanism that prepares the body to take action in the presence of perceived threat. As soon as you run into a situation that could jeopardize your well-being, this primitive part of your brain sends signals to the rest of the body to get it ready to respond to the threat. Your heart rate, your blood pressure, your breathing rate, your sweat glands, your vessels, your bladder, your muscles—they all get a message to increase or decrease their function to enable you either to fight the threat with all your might or to run in the opposite direction as fast as you can. If your brain determines that there is no threat, it deactivates the sympathetic nervous system and all the hyperactivity slows down.

The term *fight-or-flight response* was first used in 1929 by Walter Cannon to describe how animals respond to threat. Over the years, researchers studying the fight-or-flight reaction extended it to humans, and expanded it to include a sequence of four possible reactions: freeze, fight, flight, or fright.[1]

The first reaction is to *freeze*. When you run into a potentially dangerous situation, you stop what you are doing, focus your attention on the threatening stimulus, and try to figure out what to do next. If you are walking in the forest and you see a fire, you realize that you may be in danger. You stop what you are doing and focus on the fire.

Next, in the sequence is the *fight*-or-*flight* reaction. You choose whether to fight the threat or to flee from the scene. If this is a small campfire that is still burning, you will get closer and put it out. If it looks like a raging wildfire, you will run in the opposite direction as fast as you can and call for help.

If you can't find the strength to do either of those, the last kind of reaction is to stop dead in your tracks. The last response in the sequence, *fright*, is what a lot of animals do when they have a potentially fatal encounter with a predator: They play dead. They stop moving, they stop blinking, they stop breathing, and they hope that the predator will lose interest. A lot of predators will skip a meal consisting of already dead prey, because of the risks involved in eating rotten flesh. In humans, fright is like refreezing. It means doing nothing, taking no action, and just waiting passively for problems to go away.

WHEN THE BODYGUARD IS
WORKING OVERTIME

We no longer live our lives roaming in the wild, being chased by scary critters willing to eat us. These days our survival is being challenged in different ways. We worry about job stability, financial security, health and disease, social acceptance, sexual attraction, good reputation, our children's future, world peace, global warming, and a lot more. These are the modern threats.

While the threats have changed, the brain's reaction remains the same. As soon as the brain perceives threat, it activates the freeze-fight-flight-or-fright (4F) response. Confronted with something that you perceive as threatening, first, you freeze. You realize there is a problem that you need to solve. You start focusing your attention and energy into that problem to decide what to do. Depending on how serious you perceive the threat to be, you choose whether to fight it or to flee from it. And if you can't do either, you stay frozen. If you don't think you have the ability or the resources to solve the problem, you give up and wait for the problem to consume you.

For example, you heard that your company would be laying off employees. You *freeze.* You stop and listen. This is not the kind of news that you brush off. It affects you and may hurt you. Next, do you choose *fight*? Do you go to your supervisor to get more information? Do you dig up your contract or your performance evaluations to justify why you shouldn't be let go? Do you pick up your pace to demonstrate how valuable you are? Or do you choose *flight*? Do you start looking for another job, try to find out more about the severance package, and prepare to apply for unemployment? If you can't get yourself to pursue any of these actions, then you go into *fright* mode. You do nothing. You lose faith in your ability to deal with this situation. You wait until you get the pink slip or you hope that they skip you this time around.

The 4F response works well. It has been doing its job for thousands of years and has ensured that as a species we have made it safely to the twenty-first century. But here is the problem. While the system is activated automatically when you perceive threat, it is not designed to decide whether the threat is real. If you *think* you are in danger, the fear response sequence becomes activated. When you think something is dangerous, scary, impossible to handle, an obstacle, a problem that exceeds your abilities, your brain will continue to treat it that way. And that's what self-doubt is. Thinking that there is a threat and believing that there is nothing you can do about it. The physical, emotional, and mental reactions to the perceived threat are so strong that your rational brain remains quiet when the fear response is activated. Any chance of recognizing that the threat is not real is gone. And you remain in fright mode.

THE EARLY YEARS

We start perceiving the world as a dangerous place through our early experiences and interactions with others. Children learn to respond to the world emotionally through a process called *affective resonance*. When they encounter a new situation, they don't know whether they should be afraid and avoid it or whether they are safe and can enjoy it. They look up to their adult caregivers for guidance. And whatever the emotional reaction of their caregiver, that is the reaction they mimic. If a child sees a dog in the park and he has had no experience or interaction with a dog before, he will look toward the caregiver to decide if he should get closer or run back. If the adult looks calm, the child feels safe, and approaches the dog. If the adult looks frightened, the child feels fear, and moves toward the caregiver for safety. Children learn fear early, and they choose safety over experience. The fear lasts and becomes more general. The child who was once afraid of the dog may now be afraid of speaking up at work, asking for a raise, and quitting her job. When adult caregivers constantly worry and warn about the imminent presence of threat, these children will always treat the world as a dangerous place.

Children also quickly learn about the consequences of their actions. If they get in trouble, the caregivers will punish them. If they get hurt, the caregivers will be worried and upset. If they fail in school, the caregivers will be both mad and sad. Because of these negative experiences, children learn to stop taking action.

Not taking action, or playing dead, so to speak, keeps you safe. When your brain fails to suppress the fear, you continue to see threat where there isn't any and you avoid. Avoiding the threat means no risk, no exposure, no failure, no disappointment. Unfortunately, it also means no progress.

Brainblock Side Effects

The automatic response to self-doubt is to seek safety. Doing things that feel comfortable and safe. And while that may be OK when you are in the jungle fighting for your life, it is extremely limiting when fear causes you to miss opportunities to improve your life, your career, your relationships, or even the whole world.

What happens to self-doubters?

STUCK IN THE COMFORT ZONE

Self-doubt is an obstacle to learning and growth. It prevents you from taking risks. You like to stick to the familiar. The new, the unknown, and the unexplored scare you. You are torn between wanting to step outside your comfort zone and feeling safe inside it. As a result, the comfort zone doesn't expand. Its boundaries stay fixed.

However, not much happens within the comfort zone. Things stay the same. The same routines, the same activities, the same expectations, the same lifestyle. Any movement is lateral. There are no leaps and bounds, nothing extraordinary.

The cast of characters in the comfort zone also stays the same. You stick with the people with whom you feel comfortable, even though they don't challenge you and they don't help you move forward.

SHRINKING DREAMS

Self-doubt doesn't only make you hesitate to take action. It makes you hesitate to dream as well. Lacking confidence does not only keep you from taking big steps toward your goals. It also prevents you from setting big goals. Out of fear of failing, you shrink your goals to what you see as attainable.

Although setting small goals as means of attaining a large one is actually a very good strategy—you start building your tower one brick at a time—the smallness of the self-doubter's goals is not strategic. It is a cop-out. Dreaming big is prohibitive. But the cost of dreaming small is enormous. Small dreams require small actions and bring small results. What you perceive as unattainable, you will never have. And all you are left with is regrets and unfulfilled desires.

LIVING IN FEAR

There is nothing more miserable than constantly living in fear. Challenges are perceived as threats. At the slightest deviation from the safe and familiar, alarms go off and hair stands on end. The space outside the comfort zone feels like a minefield. Fear keeps you confined in the cage of security.

Fear has enormous evolutionary value. It informs you that there is real danger around you and that you need to do something. But constantly living in fear makes it useless and destructive. When you are afraid around the clock, you lose the ability to discriminate between a real threat and a harmless event. In addition, chronic fear wears your body down. Being constantly on red alert means that your entire body is on overdrive, which causes significant wear and tear on your physical and mental health.

CRUSHED BY CRITICISM

Feedback is perceived like criticism. As if lacking self-confidence were not painful enough, it makes you hypersensitive to other people's comments about you. Because of a shaky foundation, the slightest remark about your performance seems like a warning or a punishment and makes you sink a little deeper in the pool of self-doubt.

Sticks and stones may break your bones, but criticism will crush you completely. Instead of keeping your ears perked up to learn from what you are told, you cover them. And when a negative comment makes it into your head, it is amplified at deafening decibels and reverberates in there for hours. Instead of moving you to the next level, fear of criticism will keep you from moving at all.

ZERO IMPACT FACTOR

Confidence breeds confidence. A person with confidence engenders trust and confidence in others as well. Confident people are better leaders, better teachers, better parents, and better partners. Their conviction, their ability to defend what they stand for, their willingness to dream big and act even bigger are inspiring.

In contrast, self-doubters are exasperating to watch, especially when they have great potential that they are unwilling to recognize and cultivate. Their sheepishness and overused modesty are turnoffs, especially for people who are looking for role models and mentors. People don't listen to self-doubters, because they don't speak loud enough, if they speak at all. Due to their own undermining and underpublicizing of their abilities, self-doubters never earn anyone's confidence vote. At best, they earn the "just another nice guy" title.

Smashing the Brainblock

Self-doubt is caused by fear. It is triggered when the brain misfires and signals threat, when there is no real threat. The antidote is to train your brain to suppress unnecessary fear. The goal of these strategies is to increase your ability to manage fear.

To undo the automatic fear reaction, you need to "habituate" to the fear. Fear is more likely to emerge in new and presumably dangerous situations. Habituation happens when after repeated exposure to the situation, the brain no longer reacts strongly to the scary stimulus. In other words, by putting yourself repeatedly in the situations that you fear the most, you are reducing your fear, and as a result removing the brainblock.

Removing the brainblock of self-doubt means building self-confidence. Threats will no longer seem menacing, challenges will not feel like unsolvable problems, and you will never feel too "small" to deal with them.

STRATEGY 1: TOOT YOUR OWN HORN

Selling yourself to yourself is difficult because you are your hardest customer. But if you can't convince yourself about your own value, you can't convince anyone else.

Get in the habit of tooting your own horn regularly. Remind yourself of your qualities and embrace them. The three exercises that follow are intended to make you reflect on your strengths and package them in a way that will make you sound like a fierce contender. The more seriously you take them and the more thought you put into them, the more surprised you will be with the results. And feel free to share your answers with someone you trust.

....

EXERCISE 1
WRITE A PERSONAL AD

If you are currently in a relationship, write the ad as if you were trying to get your partner or spouse to go out with you on a first date. Knowing what he or she likes about you, focus on highlighting those qualities in your ad. If you are not in a relationship, write the ad to appeal to the kind of person you would really like to go on a date with. Write about yourself in a way that explains why being with you would make their life better and richer.

....

EXERCISE 2
WRITE A COVER LETTER FOR YOUR DREAM JOB

Imagine that you were preparing a cover letter for a job posting that describes your dream job. Knowing how rarely dream jobs come around, you really want this one, so you want to include in that letter all the reasons why that company should hire you and what the benefits will be for them to have you on their staff.

....

EXERCISE 3
WRITE A RECOMMENDATION LETTER

In this case, write about yourself in third person. Depending on your current life stage, either:

a. Address it to a university admissions committee, and write as if you were trying to help this person (you) get into graduate school.

b. Address it to an employer, and try to convince the employer why he should hire this person (you) for the job.

c. Address it to a landlord, a loan manager, a business partner, or any other party that this person (you) is trying to impress.

STRATEGY 2: FACE THE MONSTER

One of the most effective ways to remove the brainblock of self-doubt is to know what you are afraid of. Turning your self-doubt into self-confidence requires exploring your fears.

Dr. Karl Albrecht, author of the book *Social Intelligence: The New Science of Success*, believes that there are only five basic fears (extinction, mutilation, loss of autonomy, separation, and ego-death), and that all other fears are just variations on these five themes.[2] He defines fear as the anxiety associated with anticipating an imagined event or experience.

Based on Albrecht's work, this is my version of the five fears:

FEAR OF DYING. You are literally afraid you are going to die and that your actions are going to lead to your extinction.

FEAR OF GETTING SICK OR INJURED. You are worried you may lose or damage a body part, an organ, or function by taking action.

FEAR OF LOSING CONTROL. You worry that you will end up either physically or metaphorically locked up or restrained, that you will stop being in charge of your life and your decisions.

FEAR OF BEING ALONE. You are afraid of being rejected or abandoned by others and want to avoid becoming irrelevant, undesirable, disrespected, devalued, or disconnected.

FEAR OF HATING YOURSELF. You worry that what you do is going to cause so much shame, humiliation, or self-disapproval that it will shatter your self-esteem and self-worth.

These fears are not about the nature of our actions, but about their consequences. We hesitate to take action because we are afraid of what might happen to us. For example, Peter—our regional retail manager from earlier in the chapter—suffered from fear of public speaking. But his fear was less about speaking in public and more about what his colleagues and supervisors would think of him. Without fear of consequences, he wouldn't have frozen when he came to the podium to speak.

Therefore, to take action, you need to discover what kind of consequences you are really afraid of. Here is how to face the monster. Make a list of things that you have been too scared to do—that is, actions that you have been afraid to take. After you complete the list, do the following exercise. Pick one action. Use the worksheet on the next page and write it down.* Then go through each type of fear, and answer each of the questions with as much detail as you can, including the worst thing that could happen. Below each question is a scale that ranges from 0 to 10. This scale is your *self-power* scale. It rates your ability to handle challenges. A value of 0 means absolutely no confidence in your ability to solve the prob-

---

* You can get more worksheets and other materials for this book from my website, SmashingTheBrainblocks.com.

lem or handle the challenge, and a 10 means total confidence in your ability to solve any problem. After you identify the consequences, rate your ability to deal with them on the self-power scale by circling the number that corresponds best to how you feel right now.

ACTION

CONSEQUENCE

1. FEAR OF DYING—
   WHAT WILL HAPPEN TO MY LIFE?

   0 1 2 3 4 5 6 7 8 9 10

2. FEAR OF GETTING SICK OR INJURED—
   WHAT WILL HAPPEN TO MY BODY AND HEALTH?

   0 1 2 3 4 5 6 7 8 9 10

3. FEAR OF LOSING CONTROL—
   WHAT WILL HAPPEN TO MY FREEDOM?

   0 1 2 3 4 5 6 7 8 9 10

4. FEAR OF BEING ALONE—
   WHAT WILL HAPPEN TO MY RELATIONSHIPS?

   0 1 2 3 4 5 6 7 8 9 10

5. FEAR OF HATING YOURSELF—
   WHAT WILL HAPPEN TO MY SELF-ESTEEM?

   0 1 2 3 4 5 6 7 8 9 10

What do you notice? What are your highest and lowest scores on the self-power scale? For which questions? Were there any new insights? Did you predict any positive consequences?

As you work your way through the book, come back to this worksheet at a later time and rate yourself on the self-power scale again. You will notice that your scores are getting higher. And remember the famous words of Nietzsche: That which does not kill us makes us stronger.

STRATEGY 3: IF YOU DON'T KNOW IT, LEARN IT

Self-doubt is related to lack of knowledge. What you don't know scares you. When you are scared, you can't make informed and rational decisions. And you are more likely to hesitate to take action. Better the devil you know than the devil you don't.

A lot of people, for example, experience self-doubt when it comes to buying a used car. They worry that they will be duped by the car salesperson. They don't think they are good at negotiating, they don't know what a fair price is, they have no idea how to tell a good car from a lemon, and they don't know which brands are the most reliable. They hate having to negotiate prices with the salesperson, because they don't think they can win. They will probably sweat, hem and haw, and give in to the salesperson's first demand. But one thing that could boost anyone's confidence about car buying is knowledge. You could study the facts before walking into a dealership. Learn a few things about used cars to be able to speak and understand the language of car salespeople. Find out ahead of time what the invoice price is so you can negotiate a better price. Consult with consumer guides about used-car reliability. The more you know, the more comfortable you will be with this process.

Information gives you confidence. Dealing with facts and data moves your brain activity from the more primitive 4F system to more advanced, less emotional parts of the brain. That gives your fear responses fewer opportunities to take over and keep you stuck. Whether you are going for a job interview, starting your own business, taking an exam, going for a medical visit, or buying a house, the more you know before you go, the more confidently you will handle the situation, and the better the results will be. When you feel doubt about your ability to deal with a challenge, do your homework. Seek information. Get the facts and study them. Use any of the available resources you have at your disposal: the Internet, the library, an expert, television, the newspaper, the radio, family and friends, bloggers, professors, or a self-help book.

Think of your most important goal. Do you know what you need to do next to move toward that goal? What is the action you need to take? What kind of skills do you need? What kind of resources do you need? How long could it take? Where could you get more information? Where could you learn the skills? Who do you know who has accomplished the same goal? How did she do it? Knowing the answers to these questions alone doesn't lead to success, but it eliminates unnecessary fear, boosts confidence, and shifts your mind-set from hesitating to taking action.

STRATEGY 4: PRACTICE MAKES BETTER

Lack of knowledge or information can put a dent in your confidence. But lack of experience can drain it completely. As you become more proficient at something, you build more confidence and eliminate self-doubt.

When you lack experience you make mountains out of molehills. Speaking of public speaking, I remember the first time I had to present to a professional audience at a large conference. It was unnerving. The stakes were high, because I had just been hired and my boss was in the audience. A couple of hours before my presentation, I had angina-like symptoms so severe that I thought I would need to go to the emergency room. My stomach was queasy, my palms were clammy, and I had lost all color on my face. Talk about a 4F response! I must have rehearsed my mere ten-minute speech about thirty times that morning. Since then, I have given many presentations. Even though I still get a little anxious, I don't get angina, I don't feel like passing out, and the hours before the presentation are no longer harrowing. Now, being in front of an audience is one of my favorite ways of connecting.

In his book *Outliers*, Malcolm Gladwell points out that success is a function of extensive practice and that people at the top of the ladder in their respective fields are the ones who have thousands of hours under their belt.[3] The message? Tackle what you don't know and do it over and over and over again.

Repeated practice helps you improve your actual skills and makes them automatic. But it also gives you a taste of success as you become more proficient. That's how you build confidence. The same rule applies whether you want to become a better tennis player, a better painter, or a better money manager.

Think of your most important goal again and identify an action that you have been afraid to take. First, fill your knowledge gap (Strategy 3). Seek information, find out how you can learn more to improve the skill that you need, how much time it takes, who should teach you, and so on. Then start practicing. A lot. For hours. Be consistent, be diligent, and be open to feedback. Start tracking your progress. And finally, be surprised by the results.

STRATEGY 5: MODEL THE ONES WHO CAN

One of the best ways to defeat self-doubt and build confidence is to emulate other people who are succeeding at the things you aspire to do. An effective way of managing fear is through social or vicarious learning. Vicarious learning happens by observing others and enables us to mentally rehearse and learn what to do and how to react in risky situations, before we are directly exposed to the threat. That's why many people know how to perform the Heimlich maneuver, even if they never had to do it on someone who was actually choking.

If you want to accomplish your goals but are feeling insecure and not sure you have what it takes, start by identifying the people who are accomplished in the same way you want to be accomplished and model them. Observe what they do and learn from them.

First, think of your most important goal or your most

burning desire. Next, identify three people with similar goals and dreams to yours, who have been able to accomplish them. These people include those you know personally (friends and family), those you know of (friends of friends and colleagues at your place of business), and those who are completely unknown to you (celebrities and public figures). Write down their names:

1. _____

2. _____

3. _____

Next, start learning more about these people. Study them closely. Find out how they did it. What are they good at? How do they spend their time? What do they do for work? What do they do for fun? What do they do for personal growth? What do they read? Who do they hang out with? Who were their mentors? If these are people that you know personally, ask them if they would be willing to mentor you. If they are people you don't know personally, learn as much as you can about them. If possible, follow them on social media. Connect with them on Facebook, Twitter, or LinkedIn. Read what they read, read what they write.

And always remind yourself that if they can do it, so can you.

STRATEGY 6: STAY AWAY FROM NAYSAYERS

The worst thing for your self-confidence is to have it chipped away by people whose habit is to shoot down dreams and make gloomy predictions about the future. Affective resonance works at any age. When you are about to take an action, take a risk, or make a leap, you look around for support and validation that you are doing the right thing, that you have nothing to be afraid of, and that even if you fail, you will be able to manage. When what you receive from those around you is panic, alarm, contempt, or discouragement, you will align your own feelings to match theirs and will be filled with fear and hesitation.

Alas, not everyone around you was created to be supportive and inspiring. There are the naysayers, the people whose destiny is to shoot down ideas.

Identify the naysayers in your life and stay away from them. Naysayers are cynical, skeptical, and absolute. This is how to recognize them:

- **They state their opinions as facts.** They base their opinions not on facts or on experience, but on arbitrary assumptions.
- **They don't invite dialogue.** They don't ask questions to find out more. They don't care how important your goal is to you.
- **They don't engage in problem solving.** They won't help you find different angles to approach the situation.
- **They catastrophize.** They make arbitrary predictions that something will not work out.
- **They never say "I don't know."** They speak as experts on topics they have no idea about. They do not

admit their limitations. And what they don't know about, they consider useless.

Naysayers will fuel your self-doubt. And if you grapple with your own uncertainty, you become more vulnerable to their bites. Keep naysayers at bay. Be open to their feedback, but take it with a grain of salt. The cost of what they can do to your self-doubt is much higher than the benefit of anything you can learn from them.

STRATEGY 7: TALK THE TALK, WALK THE WALK

Sometimes you have to pretend. If you pretend, you will start believing. And once you start believing it, you will start living it.

Body language is very consistent with mind language. In other words, your body posture, your facial expressions, and your tone of voice are all informed by and related to what you are thinking and what you are trying to express. When you wince, you are in pain, when you smile, you are pleased, when you yell, you are either excited or angry.

Self-doubt affects a person's physical presence in a variety of ways. Self-doubters slouch, they retreat, they giggle nervously, they blush, they speak softly, they ask questions instead of making statements, they avoid the spotlight.

Adjusting your body language first may have an unexpected impact on your confidence levels. Research has shown that changing your facial expression, for example, will have an impact on your mood, because the brain perceives the facial expression as a sign of external or internal stimulation that is supposed to elevate or depress mood.

Talking confidently, standing confidently, walking confidently will give you an air of conviction and will also be very reassuring to others. The things that you worry about saying or doing wrong will still be wrong or right whether you do them timidly or boldly. So why not opt for boldness?

Dr. Amy Cuddy, a professor at Harvard Business School, is a firm believer that body language shapes who you are. Cuddy suggests practicing power poses. These power poses are postures that have been shown in research to boost people's confidence and to make them more appealing to other people. See her amazing TED talk, and start practicing power poses now![4]

■ ■ ■ ■ ■ ■ ■

PROCRASTINATION

Getting Things Done Sooner

Have you ever wondered why you check unimportant emails just before you start working on a project? Why you spend more time looking up weird autoimmune diseases online than doing research to find a good family physician? Why it is easier to call a friend to complain about your current employer than to start calling future employers? Why doing the dishes instead of doing a business plan seems to be the priority right now?

If there is a crime that we are all guilty of, that is procrastination. Procrastination is like the surf that eats away at the coastal rocks, very slowly, chipping away a few hundredths of an inch each time it gently licks the rocks, until one day the rocks become so jagged, porous, and unstable that they eventually collapse. Procrastination has the same effect on your goals. Every time you procrastinate, your goals become eroded, until one day they crumble before they ever had the chance to materialize.

The essential ingredient of success is action. A goal will not materialize without action. Procrastination results in delays. And delaying action eventually has the same effect as not taking action at all. Procrastination is delaying the pursuit of a goal indefinitely and with enormous consequences.

However, the real problem with procrastination is that things *do* get done eventually. You delay taking action until the last minute possible. You wait till you are dangerously close to the deadline. But eventually you get things done. And that's a problem! Why? Because it gives you the false confidence that you *can* get things done *regardless* of how late you start working on them.

Here is an even bigger problem. What happens when there are no established deadlines? What if there are no due dates? How long can you postpone something before you never get to do it?

While the cycle of last-minute pressure and I-got-it-done reward works for those tasks that have a time stamp on them, it fails in the absence of deadlines. Procrastination means that you wait till the last minute to get things done, but that works only if you know when the last minute is. When there is no clearly defined and articulated last minute, you are putting yourself in a dangerous predicament, and you don't even know it.

Life goals have no deadlines. When we are younger there are some widely accepted and relatively clear deadlines. People expect us to start teething, talking, walking, and toileting ourselves by a certain age. We are supposed to start and finish school by a certain age. Our folks may even expect us to learn the value of work by a certain age. But as we get older, the time frames become looser and more flexible. No one tells you when you should get married or get rich (unless they are your parents!). Life goals, like advancing in your career, starting your own business, achieving financial freedom, becoming the person you aspire to be, helping other people reach their goals, have no deadlines. No deadlines means no consequences. It also means no action. And no action means no results.

Hundreds of articles and dozens of books have been written about procrastination, with one and one goal only: how to stop it. So why haven't we collectively as a species stopped procrastinating already? Why are we procrastinating about getting rid of procrastination? Maybe we aren't asking the right question. Maybe how to stop it is not the problem. Maybe how it starts is the problem.

The Confessional

Alicia is a sales executive for a big media licensing company. She has been with the company for three years and is consistently one of the top performers. Between work and home life, Alicia has very little free time, so sometimes she lets things slip through the cracks. For example, back in March, she noticed that her passport was due to expire in May. Already overwhelmed with work-related stuff, the tediousness of renewing her passport seemed enormous. Because she wasn't planning to travel out of the country soon, she didn't take care of it right away. May went by, and so did June, July, and August. In mid-September, her boss told her that she needed to attend an important sales meeting in South America at the end of the month. Alicia panicked. She went home, found her passport, and kept staring at the expiry date, hoping she was wrong. She wasn't. Passports take four to six weeks to renew. For a little extra money you can speed up the process by requesting expedited service, which, as per the Department of State, takes three weeks door-to-door guaranteed! Alicia gathered the required documents, sent in the renewal application, and hoped for the best. Meanwhile, she made travel arrangements, airfare and hotel, and was keeping her fingers crossed that the passport would make it on time for her travels.

Two days before her trip, the doorbell rang, and a bubbly courier delivered a small package. The passport had arrived! The extra cost for the expedited services was worth every penny. Alicia packed her bags, made arrangements for dog-sitters, booked taxis to and from the airport, set her out-of-office notifications, and told everybody at work "see you next week!" Things worked out. Even though she waited till the last minute to renew her passport, she got it on time and was ready to go.

Only while waiting for the taxi to go to the airport did it occur to her that her tourist visa for South America was in her old passport! Luckily, the State Department sends you back your canceled old passport along with

the new one. All Alicia had to do was to take both passports with her. She went to her desk, went through her
important documents folder, and found it. She took it out
and put it together with her new passport. She opened it,
to check that the visa was still there. It was there. A col-
orful sticker, showing her photo, her date of birth, and an
expiration date of . . . last April. As her blood rushed to
her head, Alicia heard the taxi outside honking for her
to come out.

She spent the next few hours canceling flights (with
severe penalties), canceling hotel reservations (no can-
celation possible for prepaid reservations), and thinking about what she would tell her boss. Not only did she
lose money on airfare and hotel, but she lost a big commission by missing the meeting and, even worse, she put
her entire professional reputation at stake. Her oversight
of something so small was going to cost her big.

Welcome to the world of the most popular and
change-resistant brainblock: procrastination.

Spotting the Brainblock

The primary action of procrastination is *delaying*. For
how long? Who knows! That really depends on the task.
Some will be delayed indefinitely.

Primary Action:

I delay

What are the signs of procrastination?

1. YOU WAIT . . .

Until the last minute to get something done
You know what you have to do, and you know exactly when it is due. You know when the term paper is due, when your presentation for the business meeting is scheduled, and when your taxes are due. But knowing doesn't translate to doing. You wait till you are danger-ously close to the deadline.

Because you think you are good at doing things last minute
Paradoxically, procrastination makes you feel good! It has the same effect on you as a drug has on an addict! Pushed against a deadline, you engage in last-minute frenetic action. You get a strong adrenaline rush from fighting the deadline. And the fact that something that seems impossible, like finishing a paper in one night, ac-tually gets done gives you an unforgettable high! And it also boosts your sense of confidence! You get things done, even in the nick of time! You become addicted to doing things last minute!

But you wish you had an extension
You believe that you will get the work done eventually, so you put it off till the last possible minute. You underesti-mate how much time and other resources you will need to get something done, and you overestimate your ability to pull it off. You convince yourself that everything will

work out. But eventually you either run out of time or run out of energy. If only you had a little more time.

2. YOU START WORKING ON SOMETHING . . .

But much later than you intended
You don't always want to wait till the last minute. You want to start working on something as early as possible. You start thinking, you start planning, but you never start executing. The ambiguous and undefined "later" keeps moving further and further out in time, until it crashes against a deadline, if one even exists. Before you know it, you are behind schedule again.

And you end up with more worry than work
Proportionally, you spend more time worrying than getting work done. Even when you put off work for something fun, you still worry in the background. The worry increases as you get closer to a deadline, but that still doesn't translate into action.

And a lot of guilt
As if worrying weren't bad enough, you also feel guilty and make promises to never procrastinate again.

3. YOU FIND . . .

No time for the really important things
You have a lot of ideas about how to turn your life around. But you have a busy life already. You have a lot of responsibilities at work, at home, or at school. Any new ideas

require a lot of time and a lot of effort. So despite how much you would like to explore these ideas and turn them into action, they can wait; they are not a priority right now. They don't have a due date.

Plenty of time for other things
What do you do instead of working on important life-changing tasks? Filler tasks. Easy, familiar, fun tasks. Watching one more episode of that witty British series with the aristocrats and their servants instead of organizing your tax documents to hand over to your accountant. Tidying up your desk and organizing your files instead of actually writing the report for work.

Reasons to wait for the right time
You wait till the time is right, till the mood is right, till the market is right, till the weather is right. You believe that your intuition will guide you better than your sense of discipline, so you wait till the stars align.

Behind the Brainblock: Failure to Initiate Action

The number of excuses to justify procrastination is infinite: false reassurances (I will get it done), sudden shift in priorities (I had to take care of something urgent), feigned illness (I'm just not feeling well enough to deal with this today), feeble attempts for sympathy (it's not an easy task), and even self-deceptive tactics (I thought about it a little today, therefore it's almost done). But just because you can come up with great justifications for why you have not started pursuing your goal, it doesn't mean that your deed will go unpunished.

Many theories have been proposed to explain procrastination. Some of them focus on the characteristics of the avoided task. Researchers asked, Do people tend to put off some tasks but not others? Are there some specific features about the tasks that keep people from tackling them? Do people develop aversive feelings about certain tasks and find comfort in others? They discovered that tasks that people perceive as less pleasant and more confusing, stressful, and difficult tend to get pushed back.[1]

Other theories focus on the characteristics of the procrastinator. Here the researchers want to find out if there are certain personality traits that distinguish people who start late from those who start early and whether procrastination is an irreversible, untreatable character flaw. The answers to these questions seem consistent but kind of obvious: People who are less disciplined, who deliberate more, and who are not achieving much tend to procrastinate more.[2]

The truth is that both sets of theories have merit. The reason you procrastinate is a combination of who you are and what you have to do. To defeat procrastination you need to change your relationship to the action you need to take. That can happen by either changing who you are or changing the task. Changing the task—doing something other than what you see as unpleasant, confusing, and difficult—is much easier. But some tasks are unavoidable. That leaves you with only the option of changing yourself. How do you do that?

Let's take a look at what's going on inside the brain. Pursuing a goal involves many different cognitive functions. Attention, reasoning, emotion management, and impulse control all play a significant part. But the most important of them all is our executive function. Executive function is the brain's most sublime function, and an even better predictor of creativity, success, and satisfaction with life than a person's IQ. Executive function allows us to choose, plan, initiate, monitor, adjust, and stop an action.[3]

To set, pursue, and achieve a goal, the brain goes through all of these steps in sequence. Getting things done is a matter of knowing *what* needs to be done, knowing *how* to get it done, getting started, doing it, and checking the results.

Pursuing a goal successfully relies on taking action. Initiation is the most important step in the sequence of executing an action. It is the transition between planning and implementing the necessary action. Initiation is to your brain like the ignition is to your car. It is the spark plug that prepares the engine to move. When the brain's initiation mechanism glitches, you can rest assured that despite *planning*, you won't be able to start *doing*. This glitch causes a disconnection between the part of your brain where your ideas and goals are formulated with the part of the brain where action is generated. And that means procrastination. The plan fails to translate into action.

A study was done in 2011 to explore if there is a relationship between academic procrastination and executive function. The researchers approached 212 students at a large university in New York City and gave them measures to complete to assess their procrastination tendencies and their executive function. What they found was that among other things, college students who procrastinate have low initiation scores.[4]

You may have brilliant ideas, long-lasting desires, and grandiose plans percolating in your head, but without initiation there will be no implementation.

THE SEVEN PREDICTORS OF PROCRASTINATION

Procrastination is selective. You are more likely to procrastinate with some tasks but not with others. For example, you may never procrastinate checking your email, feeding the cat, making weekend plans, or paying your bills. But with other tasks, like getting your annual medical checkup, organizing your finances, or finding an executive coach, you may be the biggest procrastinator. So what changes the probability that one task gets done and another doesn't?

There are seven predictors of procrastination. These predictors are your reactions to the action you must take. Your brain responds based on your perception. Depending on how you think about the action you need to take, the probability that you will procrastinate increases or decreases. Your initiation mechanism will either shut down and get you stuck or kick in and get you in motion.

PREDICTOR 1: SKILLS

Do I Have the Essential Skills to Complete the Action Successfully?

You may realize that you don't have the technical knowledge to put together a website, realize that you don't have the management skills to run your own business, or realize that you lack the creativity to be an entrepreneur.

In terms of brain function, a skill is the memory of a well-established motor sequence—a series of body movements that are executed step by step—that your brain can activate and perform without much conscious thinking. Driving is a good example of a skill that you learn at some point in your life and that you can perform automatically for the rest of it. But imagine if instead of putting you behind the wheel of a car, someone put you behind the wheel of a speedboat. It would take you a lot longer to set the boat in motion because the skills required to drive it are different from those used to drive a car. Your brain doesn't have the required program memorized, so it will stall you.

Something similar happens when you procrastinate with other tasks. If you think that you don't have the essential skills to master a task, especially a task related to your bigger goals, your brain will stall you, and the result will be procrastination.

PREDICTOR 2: OPTIONS

What Are My Options?

Options are different actions that you can take to accomplish one or more goals. They are what you choose to do, how you choose to spend your resources. Under normal circumstances, having options prevents you from getting stuck. But there are certain situations that will cause your brain to shut down the initiation system. You are more likely to procrastinate when you have:

No options. When you see no options, you procrastinate. If you don't know what to do, you won't do anything. Without options, the brain doesn't initiate any activity.

Too many options. A large number of options causes bottlenecking in the brain. Having too many choices makes it very difficult to pick one and stick with it. A restaurant with five entrées on the menu will make it much easier to choose what to have for dinner than a restaurant with five pages of entrées.

Vague options. When your options are not concrete and specific, you will delay taking action. Vague options do not allow the brain to activate specific motor sequences to get goals completed. If I say to you, "If you want to succeed, find yourself a good mentor," it may sound good and inspiring, but what does that really mean and how do you do it? But if I say, "Call my friend, he has a lot of experience in these kinds of deals," you are more likely to follow through because you know exactly what to do.

Competing options. Your choices may be competing for your attention and for your resources. Should you work on your book or should you spend your free hour with your children? Should you spend your bonus on a training course or on a much needed family vacation? Your brain can execute only one task at a time, so it has to make a choice. As a result, some tasks get put off, because other tasks need to get done.

PREDICTOR 3: OUTCOME

Can I Predict the Outcome of My Action?
You are much more likely to put effort into something when you know whether it will pay off and what the gains will be. Not knowing how things will turn out undermines your motivation and makes you delay taking action.

If you have ever watched NBC's *Biggest Loser* you know exactly what I mean. On that show, contestants, which consist of people who are overweight or obese, are grouped in teams and compete for a prize. But to win the prize their team needs to lose weight. A lot of weight. To accomplish that goal the teams work with a personal trainer. They are put through strenuous physical challenges and they must resist temptations, like eating their favorite dessert. The team that loses the largest percentage of weight relative to what they weighed when they started is the winner. The end result, however, is not only a cash prize but also a slim and trim body. You need to watch only one season from beginning to end and you will start craving to be a contestant on the show, regardless of your current weight! Seeing the people's amazing transformation over a few months is a much more convincing way to start working out and eating well than being told by your doctor that you need to lose weight and about the cardiovascular advantages of exercise.

Forecasting a positive outcome, especially when dealing with something new and unfamiliar, leads to action. Sometimes the cost of losing a desirable outcome is a stronger motivator than the fear of punishment for not getting things done.

PREDICTOR 4: NOVELTY

How Familiar Am I with the Action I Need to Take?
Your brain is more efficient with things that you know really well. Novelty requires more effort, new learning, and better fear management, all of which can slow down the brain and block initiation. Therefore, confronted with a new and unfamiliar situation, the odds of putting things off increase exponentially. Your comfort level is lower. You don't know the best approach to the task. You can't anticipate the problems you will face. It feels like being in a foreign town without a map, without a guide, and without the language skills. You become confused, scared, and overwhelmed. You don't know where you are and which direction to take. So you just stand there.

In contrast, when you are faced with a familiar task, you know exactly what to do. You have done it before, you know the steps you need to take, you know the strategies you need to use, and you can anticipate the challenges. In other words, you have a well-established routine, and when you have a routine you are less likely to procrastinate. Your brain will carry it out automatically.

PREDICTOR 5: EMOTIONAL TEMPERATURE

How Do I Feel About the Action I Need to Take?
How you feel about a task is going to determine the chances of getting it done. There is a complex relationship between your emotions and your motivation to complete a task.

Emotions are the brain's primal response to the environment. They were developed to help the brain make quick decisions and tell the body what to do. In most situations in your daily life, the emotions you experience are not noticeable.

In some situations, however, you may experience strong negative or strong positive emotions. Strong negative emotions, like feeling scared or anxious, annoyed or angry, overwhelmed and frustrated, disappointed and unmotivated, will cause you to procrastinate. They shut down the initiation mechanism.

Strong positive emotions, well, they too can make you procrastinate, because now you just have too much energy to stay focused, think calmly, and work deliberately.

The ideal conditions to work diligently and productively are when you are in a slightly positive emotional state.

PREDICTOR 6: RELEVANCE

How Relevant Is This Action to My Goals?

Sometimes the connection between what we want and what we need to do to get it is unclear. When what you need to do appears unrelated to your goal, you depriori- tize it and put it off. You procrastinate more when you can't see how an action contributes to your goals. Rele- vance determines the importance of the action to your goal. If you've determined something is not relevant, that means it is less important, which means you experience less motivation to get it done. Many graduate students in clinical psychology hate that they have to take statistics courses because they don't plan to be doing statistical analyses when they are in the room helping their clients improve their lives. That's why training programs make statistics a requirement for students, because otherwise no one would sign up.

Businesses are now aware that their employees are a lot more satisfied and productive when they see the rele- vance of their work to the vision of the company. They perceive that their efforts contribute to a larger goal. That's why successful companies involve their employees when they create their vision statement.

Relevance, however, is hard to perceive. Many tasks fall in the gray zone of relevance. Is watching TV relevant to your goals? Well, it depends. When students in a re- search study were asked to track their activities and classify them as "Procrastinating" or "Not Procrastinat- ing," some of the tasks they mentioned were the same on both lists (for example, working, sleeping, and watching TV).[5] The action you take can be judged only in relation to the goal you set. If your goal is to update your client list, then watching TV is not relevant to your goal. But if your goal is to cut down your family's entertainment expenses, watching a movie on TV is a good alternative to spending $100 on a movie, popcorn, and soda for a family of four in one evening.

PREDICTOR 7: RESOURCES

Do I Have What I Need to Take This Action?
Getting things done is a function of the type and amount of the resources needed to take action and generate results. Resource-guzzling tasks have a higher chance of being postponed than resource-efficient tasks. It's easier to do the dishes than to do the laundry. It's easier to respond to an email than to do market research for your project. It's easier to update your Facebook status than to update your cash-flow spreadsheet. The difference between the resources you have available and the resources you need will determine the odds of procrastination.

The five major resources that you need to pursue a goal are:

TIME. How long does it take and how much time do I have?

INFORMATION. How much do I need to learn and how much information do I need to provide?

MONEY. How much money do I need, can I afford it, and what is the return on my investment?

ENERGY. How much physical, mental, and emotional energy does the task require?

SUPPORT. What kind of support from others do I need and from whom will I get it?

As your brain creates a mental budget for the amount of TIMES (time, information, money, energy, support) that you need, perceived shortages will put a halt on taking action. Hence you will put off tasks that you estimate require more time, more research (to gather information), more money, more effort (physical or mental energy), or more help from others (support) than you have available. This is why it is important to assess your resources accurately before making a decision. Overestimating the amount of resources you need will keep you putting things off. Underestimating will leave you stranded in the middle and stuck.

Brainblock Side Effects

The consequences of chronic, daily procrastination are enormous. It is impossible to estimate how much value is lost for you and for others. Because of your delays, your ideas remain locked in your head, and your intentions never translate into action. Because you are not delivering your message to the people who could benefit from it, they may drift and struggle unnecessarily. Because your project never materialized, you will always keep wondering "what if." And most importantly, your life may never change because you made *not* getting things done a bigger priority.

What happens to those who procrastinate?

DREAMS REMAIN DREAMS; SOMETIMES THEY TURN TO NIGHTMARES

Procrastination will seriously delay you from turning your dreams into reality. Procrastinators are under a magic spell. They appear oblivious to the passage of time. They practice wishful thinking and live under the illusion that there will always be opportunities to pick up in the (undefined) future. They don't realize that every day that passes costs more in terms of both time and timing. The fire under their seat is not hot enough to get them going. They confuse the optimistic "it's never too late to start" with the deceptive "I don't have to start now." Delayed decisions, postponed actions, forfeited opportunities, and missed connections with others have long-term, invisible consequences. Unfortunately, the unfounded self-reassurance that one day they will have enough time to work on their dream turns into self-pity that they never had the chance to live their dream.

THE LAND OF MISSED OPPORTUNITIES

Procrastination leaves you completely unprepared when an opportunity arises. Opportunities are serendipitous. They appear out of nowhere, often without warning, and tend to have a short shelf life. If you don't grab them, they will disappear. Life goals without assigned deadlines are very susceptible to missed opportunities. When you have put off preparing your elevator pitch for your next big project, and you accidentally run into an investor, you may lose a great opportunity to get funding because you either won't have anything to say or you will sound so incoherent that your own mother wouldn't care to fund your idea.

Alicia thought it wasn't a problem to live with an expired passport because she didn't see any reason to renew it. Even though she travels out of the country once or twice a year, she put off getting her travel documents in order. As a consequence, she lost a big commission and a great networking and business-building opportunity.

CRUSHED INTO DIAMONDS OR INTO DUST?

Procrastination will make the quality of your work suffer. It's true that the pressure of being short on time can often have a beneficial effect. The adrenaline rush that comes with it generates energy and momentum. But too much pressure turns the rush to a crash. Running against the clock will make you sloppy, careless, and prone to make mistakes.

If you think that you are capable of working under pressure and finishing a project just at the far end of its deadline, you are missing a major point. If your goal is to get something done, you can probably do it. But if your goal is to get it done *well*, then the stakes are higher. The product of your efforts should be an example of your brilliance, not your hastiness. When you wait till the last minute, you don't allow yourself time to review your work, correct errors, fix imperfections, fill in gaps, edit and polish it; you won't have the time to explore and expand your ideas further and to grow and master your skills. Regardless of the nature of your goals, giving yourself time is essential for the quality of the final product.

IT GOES ON YOUR RAP SHEET

Have you ever asked things of people and waited indefinitely for them to get back to you? Have you ever worked on a project with someone who was not pulling his weight? Do you remember how annoyed you were and how many promises you made to yourself to never work with someone like that again (unless of course this was your boss or your spouse, in which case you have no other choice)?

How likely are you to want to work with someone like that in the future? Even if his input and contribution were valuable for your project, was it worth the frustration or the extra work he created for you?

Now ask yourself, Do I want to be that person? Procrastination will brand you as someone who is unreliable. You do not want to be the person who has the reputation of never returning calls, or always getting things done late, or needing extensions, or whose work is sloppy. You do not want to be the target of other people's frustration and annoyance. You do not want to be left out of cool projects because of a surmountable brainblock. The choice is yours.

WHAT FEELS GOOD NOW WILL BITE IN THE FUTURE

The unfulfilled dreams, the missed opportunities, the poor samples of your true value, and your questionable reputation will have a serious emotional toll. Chronic, daily procrastination will be a big blow on your self-confidence. Putting something off and getting it done last minute and under pressure is going to make you feel very competent for a brief amount of time. It will also reinforce in your mind the idea that you can deliver something by a deadline. However, most of the tasks associated with fulfilling a personal goal, unlike an assigned project, do not have clearly defined deadlines. So the postponement is perennial, the tasks never get completed, and dreams never come true. But even if there is a deadline and you manage to meet it, even at the last minute, the time you spent fretting over your inability to get it started, the anguish that you experienced during the time when the project was looming over your head, and the realization that the work you did was not the best you could have done will put dents in your self-confidence. When you look back at your track record and you see nothing checked off in the "things I always wanted to do" list, you are not going to feel proud of yourself. You will feel guilt, resentment, sadness, and hopelessness.

Smashing the Brainblock

Procrastination is a powerful daily habit. To defeat it you must attack the problem at multiple levels. Before you start working on a project, you need to identify the road-blocks. You need to assess your risk of procrastinating, find where the holes are, and fill the gaps by addressing the procrastination predictors that get in the way of action. To get started, think about your most important goal. Then think about something you need to be doing to get that goal accomplished. When you identify the action or actions you need to take, go through the following questions:*

Skills. What skills do I need? Does this action require skills that I do not have? Can I learn these skills? Can I delegate tasks to someone else who has the skills?

Options. What are my options? Do I have any? Do I have too many? Are there other tasks that demand my attention? Would I rather be doing something else instead of focusing on tasks related to my goals?

---

* For a personalized procrastination risk assessment and to get your own action plan, visit my website at SmashingTheBrainblocks.com.

Outcome. Do I know what results to expect in the future? What would be a desirable outcome? How can I align my actions toward that outcome? What will happen if I don't take action?

Novelty. How familiar am I with this task? Have I done anything similar before? What parts are new to me? What can I bring to this situation that I already know?

Emotional Temperature. What emotions are getting in the way? Am I feeling too pessimistic, anxious, disappointed? Am I too excited and unable to focus? Am I overly optimistic? Do I feel guilty?

Relevance. How relevant is this task to me? How important is it for my goals? How can I make it relevant? What can I learn from this situation that may be helpful for me in the future?

Resources. What kind of resources do I need to take action? How much time (information, money, energy, support) do I need? Do I have enough resources to pursue this goal? If not, how can I find the resources?

The strategies that follow are designed to help you address each predictor separately.

STRATEGY 1: FILL THE SKILL GAP

If you notice your lack of skill in certain areas is preventing you from taking action, there are three things you could do:

a. **Learn the skill.** The simplest way of getting around a skill deficit is to learn and practice what it is that's stopping you from taking action toward your goal. For example, if better networking is what will help you advance in your career, sign up for training in networking.

b. **Delegate.** Another way to fill the skill gap is to let someone else do that which you don't have the skills to do. Most people hire someone else to do their taxes, fix their cars, and cut their hair because they don't have to learn those skills to get the job done.

c. **Refocus.** Finally, fill the skill gap by refocusing your project toward something that you actually know how to do or you are good at. If you really enjoy home decorating but you are neither trained nor inclined to get training in interior design, you can focus on learning as much as you can *about* interior design through magazines, videos, and live viewings and then blog about what you witness, without necessarily taking it upon yourself to do the work.

STRATEGY 2: NAIL THE OPTIONS

When you find yourself having *no options*—that is you either don't know what to do next or you think you have exhausted the possibilities—or when your options are *vague*, you can do one of four things:

a. **Clarify.** Be clear about what your goals are, and spend some time defining the actions you need to take with precision. For example, when you say, I would like to find another job, be as specific as you can about the type of job and the search strategies you will use.

b. **Brainstorm.** Brainstorming, which you will learn more about in the chapter on the rigidity brainblock, allows you to generate some options when you think none are available.

c. **Do research.** Find out what other people with the same goals do, in the same situation, and in the same stage of goal achievement as you. Find forums, blogs, videos, articles, and anything else you can get your hands on.

d. **Ask for help.** Find people with experience in what you would like to do and pick their brains. Invite friends, colleagues, and family members to brain-storm with you. Finally, you could also seek some for-mal training, coaching, or consultation to get clarity on what to do next.

When dealing with too many options or competing options that are pulling you in different directions, you risk multitasking. In that case, use the strategies for the brainblock of multitasking. Some other strategies to use include these:

e. **Prioritize.** Think of the most logical and most eco-nomical way of sequencing your options.

f. **Create a not-to-do list.** Procrastination is task spe-cific. You may be very diligent about getting certain things done but completely remiss about getting other things done. Think about some tasks that have little to do with your goals but you never put off (such as catching up with your favorite show on TV, updating your Facebook status, checking email, making weekend plans, working out). Put those in your *not-to-do list*. Keep this list handy, and every time you are about to engage in one of them, don't do it, but check it off your list!

STRATEGY 3: HIGHLIGHT THE OUTCOMES

When what's on the other side of your efforts remains unclear, you need to spend some time exploring and discovering. Anticipating the outcomes is one of the most important antidotes to procrastination. Strengthening your desire to fulfill your goal will keep you on track.

Thinking about your goal and longing for the outcomes do not magically make things happen. But there is a neurological advantage. Your brain starts organizing the information that you gather related to your goals in new ways. It consolidates it and combines it with already existing information. It makes you more attuned to relevant incoming information and stores it in your memory more efficiently. You start forming new ideas, considering new approaches, and building more motivation. You start to notice the gaps in your thinking and planning, the skills that you need to learn, and the resources that you need to gather. Because of all of this brain activity, you become better prepared to take action when the opportunity strikes, and you are less likely to procrastinate.

The more you think about something, the more likely that you will do something to get it.

To keep your eyes on the prize, start building the outcomes picture as vividly as you can.

a. **List the benefits.** Take out a piece of paper (or anything you like to write on) and list all the benefits that you will enjoy by accomplishing your goals. These benefits do not have to be limited to what you will gain but also how other people will benefit from your success, including your family, your friends, your clients, your students, and even humanity as a whole.

b. **Visualize.** Close your eyes and put yourself in the future that you are hoping to build for you after reaching your goals. Create a picture with as many details as you can. Place yourself somewhere mentally, in a location, an environment, and a setting of your choice, imagining the flow of your daily life after your efforts have yielded results.

c. **Observe others.** Identify the people who have achieved the type and level of success you desire and become inspired by observing their lifestyle and enjoying it vicariously (also see "Strategy 5: Model the Ones Who Can," on page 25).

STRATEGY 4: ADDRESS THE NOVELTY

New beginnings can be exciting, but they can also feel scary and awkward. The best strategies to prevent unfamiliar situations from leading to procrastination involve slowly building new routines and making new tasks part of your life. You must remember that what now seems to you new and uncharted territory can become a very familiar routine very quickly.

a. **Pencil it in.** Treat new tasks that you have been putting off the same way you treat appointments that you couldn't miss. Put them in your calendar, reserve a specific time slot, and show up! What's important is to be present, clear your schedule of anything else, and work on your project. When time is up, stop. Go back to doing something else. Keep that appointment scheduled regularly, maybe once a week, same day, same time. After a few weeks of doing it, the task will no longer be new, and it will already have a place in your busy schedule.

b. **Just start.** Pick any task, approach it from any angle, and start interacting with it in any way possible. Do not expect to finish it or to make it perfect, but simply engage with it. Once your brain engages with the task, it begins to process information, generate solutions, and launch you into action. And even if it doesn't get the entire job done, you are at least one inch closer to your end goal.

c. **Take at least one bite a day.** Make taking action toward your goal a daily priority. Complete at least one task related to your goal on a daily basis. Each day ask yourself: *What is one thing I can do today that will bring me closer to my goal?* Starting your day this way creates the right mind-set and puts your long-term goal on your agenda. At the end of the day, make sure the last thing you do before you go to bed is to check whether you took at least one action related to your goal. If you haven't, get out of bed and do any one little thing!

d. **Use an existing routine.** You can fold new activities into existing routines. The wave of habit will carry the new task along with old tasks, and what was once new and scary will become familiar and less intimidating. For example, make calling potential clients part of your morning commute to work.

STRATEGY 5: RESET THE EMOTIONAL TEMPERATURE

When your emotional temperature is too low or too high, things won't get done. When something you need to do is making you feel either overwhelmed or underwhelmed, you will avoid it and put it off.

Because of the vital role of our emotions in all other cognitive processes, and by extension their effect on goal achievement, resetting the emotional temperature is vital. Emotions may wax or wane depending on the other predictors of procrastination. For example, lack of relevance may undermine your motivation, and lack of time may increase your anxiety. Therefore, to stay on track with your work, rely on other predictor-specific strategies to change the emotional intensity or dullness that gets in the way.

Being overwhelmed is related to running out of resources, being a novice, lacking skills, or having competing options. The strategies that will work best when you are overwhelmed are those that focus on breaking down goals, taking small bites, and not doing it on your own (see Strategies 1b, 2d, 4c, and 7c in this chapter).

Being underwhelmed is related to lack of excitement or the lack of perceived importance between what you need to do and what you would like to accomplish. The strategies that will work the best are those pertaining to explicating the outcomes (Strategy 2 in this chapter) and finding the relevance (Strategy 6, discussed next).

STRATEGY 6: FIND THE RELEVANCE

It is hard to get started on anything if you don't see the relevance of your work to the outcomes you expect. To prevent procrastination you need to discover the connection between the two. While Strategy 3 is designed to remind you of the outcomes you expect and to keep you motivated, this strategy is about making the relationship between the action and the goal clearer.

a. **Keep a log of actions.** When you are in the planning phase of a goal or a project, make a list of all the tasks you can think of that pertain to that goal (see also Strategy 7c in this chapter). Save it somewhere. Every time you question why you are doing something, check your list. If that task is in there, you are good. If it is not, go to Step b.

b. **Check your not-to-do list.** If what you are doing is on your not-to-do list, you are getting off track. Remember, tasks on your not-to-do list are the fun options that are more tempting to do than actual work.

c. **Draw lines between _A_ and _B_.** If you are a conceptual thinker, create a mind map to visually show the relationships between the tasks and your goal. When you are unclear about how a task relates to a goal, go to your diagram and see how it fits in.[*]

d. **Generalize the benefit.** When you cannot see the relevance between your tasks and your goals (for example, when your boss assigned you a task), think of how what you are doing could benefit you in the future (see also "Strategy 2: Find the Gem," on page 213).

STRATEGY 7: BUDGET YOUR RESOURCES

Determine ahead of time how much you will need and how much you have available in terms of your resources.

a. **Estimate your needs.** Figure out how much of each resource you need to complete a task or a project. Create a flexible budget sheet:

- Time. *How long will this task or project take and how much time do I have available?*
- Information. *How much do I need to learn or research? How much information do I need to provide?*
- Money. *How much money do I need? Are there recurring expenses? Is it within my budget? What is the return on my investment?*

---

[*] For an example of how to use a mind map, check out the procrastination mind map that I created when I was working on this chapter, at Smashing TheBrainblocks.com.

- Energy. *How much physical, mental, and emotional energy does the task require?*
- Support. *What kind of support from others do I need and from whom will I get it?*

b. **Set target dates.** Get in the habit of setting deadlines. Deadlines give structure to chaos. Think of deadlines as target dates that will help you stay focused and organize your time better. As you break down a goal into manageable tasks (see Strategy 7c below), set a target date for each task. Having a time stamp will engage your brain in planning and preparing for action, even when you are not actively thinking about a task.

c. **Divide and conquer.** Break down multistep actions into small, manageable tasks. Make a list of your big goals (such as write a book, change jobs, get married, start my own business). For each one create a list of all the different tasks you think are necessary to reach your goal. Keep adding to, making changes, or deleting from the list as you gain more knowledge and become more familiar with what you need to achieve your goal. Prioritize your tasks based on your available resources, and don't forget to set target dates!

d. **Set limits in stone.** Be firm about how much you are willing to expend. Read more about this strategy in "Strategy 6: Set Limits in Stone," on page 179.

■ ■ ■ ■ ■ ■ ■

IMPATIENCE

The False Sense of Urgency

They say that good things come to those who wait. But they also say seize the day or do not wait until it's too late. Which is it?

Folklore and literature are full of characters who exhibit remarkable patience in the face of serious trials and tribulations. Penelope, for example, Odysseus's wife, waited patiently for twenty years for her husband to return from the Trojan War, according to Homer's *Odyssey*. Why did she wait that long? She could have easily been with someone else. When word got out that Odysseus was nowhere to be found, forty of the best eligible bachelors of the kingdom of Ithaca set eyes on Penelope (and her inheritance!). All of them were willing to marry her; some of them were probably quite good-looking, some maybe rich, and some even smart. But she kept stringing them along, while she waited for her beloved to return to Ithaca. And he did!

Impatient people, on the other hand, don't like to wait. To them twenty minutes is too long, let alone twenty years. Why can't they wait? Don't impatient people want good things to happen to them too? Or are they better at getting what they want faster than everyone else?

A critical component of success is timing. Time your action too late, and you will miss opportunities. Time it too early, and you will be shooting arrows when the target hasn't been set up yet. Time it right and wait.

The paradox with impatience is that unlike the other brainblocks, which slow down action, impatience generates more action than necessary. We saw how procrastination delays action and self-doubt prevents it completely. But with impatience you simply can't hold back the action. You *do* make a move. Alas, you move too soon, with very little planning and without much forethought.

The key to being unstoppable is knowing when to stop. When impatience starts to kick in, action erupts. You give yourself no time to make a plan, to consider the pros and cons, to estimate the kind and amount of resources you need, to explore alternatives, to track your progress, and to fix your mistakes. As a result, you take uncalculated risk or abandon a good plan, just before you are about to reap the benefits.

The symptoms of impatience are not easy to spot. Impatience hides behind feelings and actions that make you feel good. It creates momentum and generates energy. It makes you feel spontaneous and adventurous. It makes you look efficient and demanding. It makes you a go-getter and a chop-chopper. It marks you as the person who gets things done.

Then why is impatience a problem?

The Confessional

Wealth creation courses and seminars are a breeding ground for impatience. If you have never taken one, you should, but make sure you leave your wallet at home. The organizers will present you with incredible and fail-safe wealth-building techniques. They will have you think about your biggest dreams and most desired goals. And since a lot of these dreams involve beach houses, yachts, convertibles, and margaritas by the pool, the way to make them a reality would be to have very deep pockets. They will promise that their method could help anyone build a worry-free life, have a happy retirement, and constantly commit acts of generosity. And buying their program is the only way to get there *fast*.

There is no better way to lure you into the trap of impatience than telling you that you can have what you want faster. A call to action that would open the door to your dream life will have your wheels spinning. In these seminars, the attendees are sitting at the edge of their seat waiting for instructions to start running toward their dream. The back of the room is lined with long tables manned by friendly staff ready to put you on the express track to wealth. As soon as the presenter utters the phrase "if you would like to purchase this program," everyone starts running toward the back. The friendly staff start exchanging order forms for credit cards, and they give the attendees gift bags filled with the keys to abundance.

Rosy was one of those people. Rosy ran a sluggish real estate business that she wanted to grow and make super-profitable, super-fast. She had a lot of energy, a lot of ambition, and a lot of hope. Knowing that she needed help from the experts, she signed up for a Get Rich Quick live event. There were many great presenters at the event, and one after the other demonstrated their amazing, proven techniques of making money fast. One of them in particular piqued Rosy's interest. This man had created a very reliable source of massive passive income by buying and selling . . . virtual land. He had developed a business that bought and sold domain names. Domain names are the web addresses that you type in your browser to get to a specific website (for example, SmashingTheBrainblocks.com, bmwusa.com, and msnbc.com). The most typical way to get a domain name for your website is to contact an Internet domain registrar/web-hosting company (like Bluehost or Go-Daddy), check to see if the domain name is available, and if it is, buy it (or rather rent it, and pay a recurring fee every year to maintain it, if you still need it). Registering a domain name is very easy. It takes seconds, and it costs no more than a few dollars. However, finding the domain name that you like is the real pain. If your name is James Smith or Maria Garcia (two of the most popular first/last name combinations) and you would like to create a

website and use your name as the web address, you are
out of luck. About thirty thousand Jameses and Marias
have already tried before you, also without luck. So the
idea behind domain trading is to buy a web address
cheaply, and if someone else wants it badly at a later
point in time, sell it to them at a much higher price.[*] It's
almost like swapping fixer-uppers. The idea of making
money so easily by trading virtual real estate was very
appealing to Rosy. After forty-five minutes, she knew she
had to buy this training program. She went to the back of
the room, gave her card to the friendly staff, got her receipt, and went back to her seat, confident that she had a
reservation on the express train to wealth.

Two days later, reality struck. Rosy was staring at the
receipt for this extravagant purchase, lamenting what
she had done! How could she have spent so much money
on something that was so misaligned with her goal of
growing her business and, worse, that she wasn't even
very interested in doing? She looked at the return policy.
Either cancel within three days for a full refund or say
good-bye to a big chunk of change forever. She was just a
few hours away from losing money instead of making
more! She called the number on the receipt form right
away. No answer. She emailed. No response. It was a
weekend. She waited till Monday to call again. She left a
message. Days later her call was returned and she was
told that the cancellation period had expired. She got

---

[*] Facebook, for example, paid $8.5 million in 2010 to buy the domain name
fb.com, according to *Inc.* magazine.

stuck with a program that she never needed and would never use and a credit card bill that she had to pay off. Rosy's impatience cost her. It cost her time and it cost her a lot of money. I wish I could tell you that Rosy is the only person I know who has done something like this, but I have many such stories to share! Some involve getting rich fast, others finding a cure fast, and others turning lives around fast.

Spotting the Brainblock

The primary action associated with impatience is *rushing*. Moving forward, pushing through, getting things done, not being held back. No boundaries, no filters, no brakes!

Primary Action:

I rush

What are the signs of impatience?

1. YOU ARE SPONTANEOUS . . .

You act on impulse
You do things out of pressure, without much deliberation. As soon as you think about something, you have an irresistible urge to do it. You give yourself little time to consider the reasons behind your actions and almost no time to consider the consequences. You see something

that you like online? You buy it. You have a joke in your head that you think is hilarious? You say it. You think the cupcake looks delicious? You eat it.

You find making plans limiting

Very often, you act without a plan or, even worse, despite a plan. Plans slow you down. They kill spontaneity. They kill creativity! The result? You start working on a project without a well-defined plan. But even if you do have a plan, you stop following it in the right sequence. Your timing is off, you jump from one part of the plan to another, and you even skip steps.

You are too excited to be thorough

The pressure and excitement of getting something done leaves you no desire to be thorough. Patchiness, incomplete ideas, mistakes, and omissions become trademarks of your work. If you are following a recipe, you may forget to add one of the ingredients. If you are writing an article, you may leave it full of typos. If you are sending an email, you may accidentally send it to the wrong person. Rushing is not compatible with verifying.

2. YOUR TIME IS EXTREMELY VALUABLE . . .

You like quick results

You are the biggest consumer of "Get ——— Quick!" products and services. Titles that grab your attention include Get Rich Quick, Lose Weight in Three Hours, Get Ripped in Two Minutes a Day, Increase Your IQ in a Week! Anything that comes with a disclaimer that it takes six to twelve months to work, you leave on the shelf.

And you hate slow results

When you don't get the desired results as quickly as promised, you get very disappointed and give up. You are ready to try something else that promises even faster results. You either become a junkie of quick methods or you crash and quit trying to achieve your goal.

You also hate slow people

Slowness irritates you. Long lines, slow traffic, unanswered emails, unreturned phone calls are driving you nuts. You keep checking and rechecking emails, texts, voicemail, website traffic, bank accounts, as if the world could have changed in the two minutes since you last checked.

You don't understand why delayed gratification is a desirable option

Delayed gratification is the ability to wait to receive a large reward for your efforts in the future than for a small reward in the present. Who came up with this concept? Who in their right mind would give up something now for some vague promise in the future? A bird in the hand is worth two in the bush. Life is short, why wait for tomorrow when you can have something today?

3. LIFE IS MOVING TOO FAST . . .

You are constantly fighting life's clock

You always feel like you are running behind life's schedule. You believe you should have accomplished much more by now. Time is running out, and you are far from the finish line. You actually worry that you should have been at the finish line a long time ago. Other people always seem to have accomplished more than you. You often ask yourself "Why am I not there yet?"

And you are getting older
You worry that you've run out of time and it's too late for you to achieve your goals. You are too old to start all over again, it's too late to start learning new things, you are not in a position to compete with all the younger people out there. You fear that your window of opportunity is closed forever.

Meanwhile, everything seems urgent
Your life feels like an emergency room. You can't triage because everything seems urgent. Everything requires immediate action. Waiting becomes unbearable. You start getting antsy, edgy, and panicky. You need to act fast. And while you exaggerate the consequences of not acting quickly, you seriously minimize the consequences of acting prematurely.

Behind the Brainblock:
Failure in Response Inhibition

EFFICIENCY: THE MOTIVE BEHIND IMPATIENCE

Your brain can process things fast or it can process them accurately. These two qualities, *speed* and *accuracy*, are always in competition. As one goes up the other goes down. You can either do things fast or you can do them well. Under normal circumstances, it is impossible to increase both your speed and your accuracy.

Efficiency is the ideal balance between speed and accuracy. It refers to the highest speed at which you can process information without making mistakes. Imagine that you're reading an interesting article in your favorite magazine. Efficiency is the length of time it takes you to finish reading the article and to also understand the content. If you read it faster than your brain can process, you will miss some of the information in the article, you will not pick up some of the details, and you will forget it faster. If you slow down and read it at a more leisurely pace, you will process, understand, and remember the information in the article much better. But you may be late for work!

Impatience happens when you favor speed over accuracy. Instead of taking your time, you choose to do things quickly. Instead of waiting for things to fall in place, you want things to happen faster. But inevitably, doing things faster increases the chances of making more mistakes, which you have to go back and fix.

Why would you choose to do things fast instead of doing them accurately, when doing them fast creates more work for you? Is there something that prevents you from slowing down and taking your time and still being efficient?

RESPONSE INHIBITION: THE BRAIN'S BRAKES

The neuropsychological process that lies beneath impatience is called response inhibition. Response inhibition refers to the brain's brakes. Anatomically, it is located in the frontal lobes of the brain and it is one of the most important functions for goal achievement and success. Response inhibition is a complex mechanism that decides whether action is required or not. It is the function that gives you the ability to stop yourself from doing or saying what's really on your mind.

Imagine that you are sitting in front of your computer screen. A number of words start flashing on your screen, one at a time. You are asked to read each word and press the space bar if the word follows the rule. Let's say that the rule is to press the space bar if the word starts with a vowel, but not to press it if it starts with a consonant. You are asked to respond as quickly as you can after you see the word. At the end of the test the number of times you pressed the space bar is counted. The number of times you pressed the bar when you were not supposed to (such as when the word *success* appeared on your screen) is a measure of how well your brain's brakes work. The brakes control your ability to hold back action.

Response inhibition is what allows you to ask your boss when she announces a new policy she wants to enforce, "Should we consider the pros and cons of this policy before we make it a standard procedure?" instead of saying, "This is the stupidest thing I've heard in years!" It is what keeps you from smacking the person in the movie theater sitting behind you, who thinks he was invited to add commentary aloud to the action movie you are watching. It is what stops you from changing lanes on the highway without slowing down and checking for on-coming traffic or hitting the person who just cut ahead of you in line.

When response inhibition works well, you make smart choices. You are deliberate and cautious. You plan and prepare. You do not sacrifice accuracy for speed. But like all brain activity, response inhibition is also prone to glitches. When response inhibition fails, you start show-ing signs of disinhibition. Disinhibition is the failure to suppress action. It is the failure to put the brakes on. It is the inability to stop yourself from saying or doing things that should be left unsaid or undone. It is the lack of abil-ity to make and stick to a plan.

Disinhibition happens when the brain's brakes are not quick or strong enough to stop the momentum of an impulse. The impulse pushes through the barriers, ac-tion slips out, and you become impulsive. Impulsivity can take many forms. It can be verbal (speaking out of turn or saying something inappropriate) or physical (crossing the street while the light is still red), mental (having intrusive and unpleasant thoughts, like I want a chocolate chip cookie now or I'm going to explode) or emotional (feeling irritable and annoyed or exuber-ant and bouncy). Impatience is the daily manifestation of impulsivity. It is like a surge that builds up as the impulses—whether they come in the form of words that need to be said, desires that need to be fulfilled, or ges-tures than need to be executed—can't be stopped by the mental brakes. When the impatience surge has enough force, the impulses escape into the world in the form of action.

Brainblock Side Effects

Impatient people suffer. Their inability to harness their impulses makes life an emotional roller coaster. Words and actions rise up like vomit that they can't hold down. When their premature actions don't lead to the desired results fast, they suffer more. But it is not only they who suffer. The quality of their work suffers, their relationships suffer, and even their bank accounts suffer.

What happens to those who cannot wait?

HASTE MAKES BIG WASTE

When you become impatient, waiting and wasting time becomes unbearable. To stop the suffering, you try to save time by doing something faster. But working faster means that you make more mistakes, because our brains can do things either quickly or accurately. Then you have to go back and fix the mistakes, which means double the time and double the effort.

Impatience causes careless mistakes or tactical mistakes. Careless mistakes are bound to happen when you do something fast. You don't look over your work, you don't have time to get feedback, and you don't take time to make changes. Your work seems sloppy and you appear inefficient. Careless mistakes will cost you time, money, and credibility. Tactical mistakes are a result of poor planning and lack of strategic thinking. You do things haphazardly and out of sequence, without a well-articulated and specific plan. Tactical mistakes can prevent you from achieving your goal entirely.

GIVE UP AND SETTLE FOR LESS

How long does it take to reach your goals? Two weeks? Ten months? Thirty years? Unfortunately, there is no recipe that says to leave your dreams in the oven for forty-five minutes and then take them out, let them sit for five minutes, and they are ready to eat. If you cannot handle the waiting game, you will give up before the waiting time is up. If you are impatient, you always feel late and behind schedule. If you see no immediate results, you start believing that your idea is a worthless venture and your actions were hopeless. When having to choose between what may lie ahead in your future and what is available to you right now, you will be tempted to go for the immediate reward. Why wait for the unknown, the unsecured, the imagined when you can grab the safe bet?

This is what distinguishes visionaries and great entrepreneurs from the rest. They practice patience and they aim far. They take their time to plan their launch and wait calmly for their spear to reach the target. If you are not willing to wait, you will aim for the target closest to you. Easy targets get small prizes.

WIN THE UNPOPULARITY CONTEST

Impatient people don't work well with others. When you don't have the ability to wait, you can't be patient with those around you. You perceive them as slow, inefficient, and incompetent. You get irritated and miffed, you become snippy, and you say or do things that you can't take back. Snap judgments and snarky remarks make you come across as condescending and offensive. You risk being labeled the customer from hell, the office bitch, or a plain old big jerk. You do not get picked by anyone to play on their team. People will go out of their way to avoid you.

And your impatience doesn't only affect your social life or your relationships at work. It can also kill your love life. Impatience doesn't make you a popular companion! Being unpredictable and taking uncalculated risk—typical signs of impatience—make you an unreliable partner, an unbearable spouse, and a crummy parent.

BAD FOR YOUR HEALTH

Being impatient also puts your health at risk. Several psychological studies have shown that low patience leads to poorer physical and mental health.[1] When researchers compare people based on patience, they find that those with low patience are at higher risk for developing cardiovascular disease, have lower self-esteem, set lower achievement standards, and have fewer friends and social supports.[2] Patient people, on the other hand, have much less anxiety, don't get depressed easily, have fewer health problems, and are better at helping other people.

Research on stress suggests that it hurts your physical and mental health more to have to deal with hassles and frustrations day after day than to deal with a major crisis.[3] Being impatient, and getting irritated and frustrated with small, daily delays, like slow traffic, lax customer service, or people who don't respond to your emails within minutes, can eat you up and take a toll on your well-being.

Smashing the Brainblock

Impatience involves strong emotional reactions, which are hard to miss but also hard to harness. To defeat impatience you must learn to resist your urge to jump the gun; instead, take the time to measure twice to cut once and find a balance between doing things fast and doing them well.

STRATEGY 1: BEAT THE WAITING GAME

Part A: Be Present in the Present
You become impatient when your brain needs something to do but there is nothing to do. Waiting for something to happen is one of those times. Idle waiting time is a breeding ground for impatience. There are many occasions during the day when you have no choice but to wait. Whether in traffic, at the doctor's office, in line, or online, things move slowly and you are stuck doing nothing. A

lot of your time is eaten up waiting for a response, waiting for a service, waiting for clearance, waiting for results. And when you start thinking about how late you are, what else you could be doing instead, and how much time you are wasting, the impulse toward taking action starts rising. Your brain needs an action outlet. Pretty soon, you start showing all the signs of impatience. A surge of energy in your body makes you breathe faster, fidget more, tap your feet louder, turn red in the face, and start murmuring obscenities under your rapid breath.

The best way to manage the wave of impatience is to divert its energy surge elsewhere, so you can beat the waiting game. The next two strategies are different ways to occupy your brain during idle waiting time, to prevent impatience that may lead you to impulsive actions.

When your brain needs action but what it wants to act upon is not available, you start to focus on the absences—what's *not* there or what's *not* happening. You focus on what you don't have (a response to your email, which was sent two hours ago), where you are not (at home watching *Game of Thrones*, instead of being stuck in the subway), and who is not there (your husband, who promised to pick you up from work ten minutes ago).

At times like these, you have to train your brain to do nothing. Just to be present in the moment, without taking any action. One of the best practices for being present is mindfulness. There are many definitions and variations of mindfulness that range from focusing on what's happening around you to enlightened meditation. But to keep things simple, let's define mindfulness as being aware of what is happening in your internal (your body) and your external (around you) environment. Let me give you an example. Right now, you can focus on what you are reading; you can focus on the ideas in the book, your reactions to what you are reading, or the distracting thoughts about what you will have for dinner. You can also focus on the individual letters on the page and how they are transformed into words with meaning. You can also focus on the way your fingers gracefully flip the pages, how the texture of the paper feels against your skin, how the brightness of your e-reader screen gently hits your eyes, and how your body feels against the chair that gently supports your body weight. Or you can focus on your evening plans, your upcoming deadlines, and all sorts of things you should be doing instead of reading this book, all of which are things that you don't have now. And the more you focus on those, the more impatient you will become with reading the book.

The simplest mindfulness exercise to stay grounded in the present and suppress the need for action is breathing. There are many breathing techniques, some for relaxation, some for tension release, some for symptom relief, and some for alertness.[4] A search on Google or You-Tube will give you many resources for learning and practicing breathing exercises. You can also download breathing apps on your phone. The one I use with my clients is called Breathe2Relax and was developed by the National Center for Telehealth and Technology of the Department of Defense. Mindfulness at your fingertips!

The simplest, easiest, and fastest way to use breathing to be present is this: Close your eyes and focus on your breathing. Notice the air flowing in and out. Notice how long it takes, how deep it goes, and how your body reacts. Don't change it, don't push it, don't force it. Just keep your eyes closed and notice your breath.

Now open your eyes and go on to the next strategy.

STRATEGY 2: BEAT THE WAITING GAME

Part B: Capitalize on the Present; Reap in the Future
I fly overseas at least twice a year to see family. As an experienced long-haul flyer I can tell you this: When all you can think about during the flight is, Are we there yet? you will have a miserable traveling experience. The flight seems so much longer to me when I constantly keep checking the time, looking at the screen with the flight information to see how much longer we have left, and asking the flight attendant what the expected arrival time is. My solution to this problem is to use the flight time to write. As soon as we reach the required altitude and the captain makes the announcement about portable electronic devices being allowed, I take out my laptop and start writing. In fact, I wrote about 30 percent of this book on airplanes (and a little bit on trains, but never in a car). I get so much into the writing that I barely notice that I am confined in a tight seat far away from the ground. And time seems to fly faster than the plane. By capitalizing on the present, a long flight no longer seems like wasted time between point A and point B. For me,

it has become one of the places where I am the most productive.

Another way to beat the waiting game is to give your brain something to do. Something that capitalizes in the present and will benefit you in the future. In other words, during the long, idle, and impossible-to-escape waiting moments, do something useful. Instead of focusing on how slow the traffic is, how much time the doctor is taking with the previous patient, or how long the line is till you get to the counter, focus on something else. Here are four types of things you can do while waiting:

- **Entertain yourself.** Read a fun book, listen to music on your phone or MP3 player, draw something, or play a game on your phone.
- **Learn something.** Read a nonfiction book, listen to a podcast on a topic that interests you, read the newspaper, or watch a TED talk on your tablet.
- **Plan your day.** Check your to-do list, prioritize the tasks in it, and put them in your calendar.
- **Complete mini-tasks.** Put the dishes away, take out the garbage, make quick calls, and send brief emails.

Now, while this technique works well when you have to wait to get something done pretty soon, it also works well when you have to wait for your long-term plans to come to fruition. Plans take a while to materialize. But between taking a step now and having to wait to take the next step much later, you can get very impatient. Beat the waiting game by preparing for the next step, filling in gaps, learning more, and ensuring that you are not giving up.

STRATEGY 3: MAKE A CHOICE—
TO BE FAST OR TO BE GREAT?

Trading speed for accuracy is a decision you are called to make daily and for anything you do. Some tasks require speed. Doing them fast is far more important than doing them well. For example, when you are taking notes during a meeting, writing things down fast is more important than maintaining good penmanship. You shouldn't care about grammar, syntax, or word choice. You just need to save the ideas before you lose them. You can fix the language later. If you take the time to create full and legible sentences, you will miss half of what was said at the meeting.

Other things, however, are better off done well than done fast. If you are sending your résumé to a headhunter in response to a job lead, it is much more important to take the time to go through the document with a fine-tooth comb, to make sure there are no typos, no inconsistencies, no omissions, no layout problems, than to send it in a couple of hours early and unedited.

The same rule applies to the majority of health-related decisions. Weight loss, for example, is the number one goal for a large number of people. It always comes up first in surveys about goals and New Year's resolutions. There are ways to lose weight fast and there are ways to lose weight well. What is the difference? Fast means unhealthy and unsustainable. It means putting your body through regimens that are biologically perverse, like starving it and depriving it of important nutrients and energy. It also means that you will regain the weight sooner or later because a quick weight loss method is not meant to be a lifelong eating pattern. But if beach season is dangerously close, what choice do you have but to speed it up and shed off those pounds as quickly as you can?

To prevent your impatience from making you step more on the gas pedal and less on your brakes, remember to always ask yourself before you take an action, Is it better to do this *now* or is it better to do it *well*?

STRATEGY 4: TAKE STEP ONE
BEFORE YOU TAKE STEP FIVE

Do you know what contributes to the making of a delicious dish? It isn't being a great cook. It is following the recipe accurately. Even if you have all the ingredients and in the right proportions, the dish will not turn out well unless you follow the instructions step by step. The same is true if you ever tried to put together a piece of furniture from IKEA. You have to look at the instructions, and follow them in the right sequence, unless you want to end up with a Frankenstein's monster of a bookshelf.

Life goals can have the same fate. Unless you take the steps in the right order, the goal will remain a dream.

Pursuing a goal successfully relies on having a plan. And while having a plan is great, following it is even greater. And following it step by step is the greatest.

Impatience makes it hard to stick to a plan. You spend more time looking for shortcuts than staying on track. You take step one and then go straight to step five before you take steps two through four. You start reading line ten of your recipe before you execute line three. And while this may be a good antidote for procrastination because you never delay taking future steps, doing things out of order can make a good plan implode.

If you want to make dinner, you check whether you have all the ingredients you need; if not, make a list, go to the grocery store, come back, and then proceed cooking. You do not turn on the oven first, and then check to see if you have enough phyllo dough to make spanakopita. If you need a new set of speakers for your TV set, first you may browse different websites to identify the speakers you like, then read reviews, check the specifications to make sure they are compatible with your TV, and place your order. When you are impatient, you get too excited about the product or too anxious that someone else may buy it before you, and you rush ahead. Following a plan to make spanakopita or to buy speakers is pretty concrete. But when the order of a long-term plan, like writing a book or starting a business, is disordered, the stakes are much higher. When do you write? When do you pitch? When do you market? When do you call yourself an author?

STRATEGY 5: MULTIPLY YOUR TIME LINE BY THREE

When you procrastinate, you delay. You extend your timeline indefinitely and you never get started. When you commit impatience, you rush. You create unrealistically short deadlines that you risk never making.

Research on delayed gratification shows that people underestimate how long it takes to complete something. They are pretty bad at calculating the time it will take to finish a project, especially when they really want to reap the benefits. The more you want something to happen, the more you underestimate how long it will take you to make it happen. How long do you need to make your business profitable? How many years must you spend in an entry-level position before you get a promotion? How long will it take you to put together a mortgage application?

When you fail to achieve a goal within your expected time frame, you get impatient. Then impatience turns to annoyance, frustration, disappointment, surrender, and you already know the rest.

So to harness your impatient brain, and remain calm, focused, and committed, do the following: Estimate how long it will take you to do a certain task. For example, if you are planning to apply for a small business grant to fund your home-based start-up, decide how long it would take you to write the grant. If you say fifteen days, then take that number and multiply it by three. Make the target date forty-five days. Even if that seems too long or excessive, give yourself the extra time. Then start working on the project as if it were due in fifteen days. That is, spend the same amount of time and energy that you would if the target date were closer. The worst that can happen is that you finish your project ahead of time and you have extra days to polish it or to devote the time to something else.

STRATEGY 6: MASTER DELAYED GRATIFICATION— WAIT AND YOU SHALL RECEIVE MORE

Good things come to those who wait. But in a fast-paced culture submerged in consumerism, easy solutions, and fast food, waiting seems like a hassle. Quick and easy is the reason why the junk food industry is so profitable, why people are neck-high in consumer debt, and why one in ten Americans is on a quick-fix mood drug.

Practicing delayed gratification will help you exercise your patience muscle and defeat impatience. Being able to resist the temptation for a quick fix, the low-hanging fruit, and the easy way out will be a valuable skill to have for any goal you set out to accomplish. Start practicing delayed gratification today, with the little things, so that you can increase your capacity for the larger things.

Try this exercise. Identify something small that you would really like to have available to you right now. Is it eating ice cream? Buying a pair of shoes? Watching your favorite drama series on TV? For the next few minutes think about the thing you want to have. Here is your challenge: Don't do anything about it now. Don't go to the freezer, don't go to Zappos, and don't go to Hulu Plus. Instead, set a future date to reward yourself with one or all of these treats. In the present, shift your attention to a task that is related to your future goals. Go to your to-do list, pick one task, and start working on it. Set a time limit if necessary. Give yourself the treat only on the designated date, and only after you have completed the task. That is what practicing delayed gratification feels like! Waiting now, so you can receive more in the future!

STRATEGY 7: STOP
(AND BREATHE, COUNT, OR SING A SONG)

When you become impatient, your brain gets "hot." It gets hijacked by emotions like anger or excitement, which cause a strong sense of restlessness that spreads to the rest of your body. Your blood starts rushing to your head, your face gets flushed, your heart starts beating faster, and your breathing becomes rapid and shallow. At this state, you are ready to launch into action or, rather, into attack!

To prevent an explosion, let your brain cool off. First, you have to *stop*. Literally stop. Don't do anything, don't say anything, don't move, don't even blink! Stay still, even if for two seconds. To be able to stop yourself requires a lot of willpower and discipline. The following four techniques will help you succeed:

- **Think STOP!** Say that to yourself, in your head, using your inner voice.
- **Say STOP!** Say that to yourself aloud, as if you were talking to someone else.

- **See STOP!** Use a visual cue. It could be a big red stop sign or a sticky note on your desktop with the word *stop* printed in block letters.
- **Hear STOP!** Ask someone you trust to tell you to stop when they see that you are starting to get impatient.

After you stop, engage in something that will help you blow off steam, without blowing up:

a. **Fresh air.** Take a few deep breaths. Breathing is one of the most effective techniques used for stress management and relaxation. Not only does it require that you focus on your breathing instead of acting out impulsively, but it also nourishes your brain with oxygen, which makes it work better for you.

b. **Numbers.** Many people create distance between themselves and the annoyance that the surge of impatience causes by simply counting numbers. You could count to ten, count backward from one hundred, count odd numbers, add or subtract, and so on.

c. **Mantras.** Choose a phrase that helps you refocus your attention on the present moment, on what is physically in front of you. Say it to yourself, over and over. I personally prefer to sing songs. My favorite when I need to cool down is "Slow Ride" by Foghat (take it easy!).

MULTITASKING

Once Upon a Time
There Was a Skill . . .

And that skill was called multitasking. For many years, multitasking was revered as the ability that any self-respecting and productive person should possess. Being "good at multitasking" was a must on anyone's résumé. People bragged endlessly to their employers, to their friends, and to their families about their ability to multi-task. Men and women, the old and the young, employees and their bosses, college students and their professors, athletes and coaches, artists and patrons, everyone wanted to be good at multitasking.

But suddenly, people started noticing serious side effects. They started complaining that they couldn't focus, they couldn't get things done, they were restless and tired, and their mind was racing. They felt unproductive and underperforming. Some even went to doctors to get help. Was all the bragging about multitasking just a masked cry for help? The doctors, not knowing what this was and what to do, gave it a name: adult ADHD (attention deficit/hyperactivity disorder). And a new disease was born out of an old habit.[*]

People were left with two choices: Stop multitasking or take a pill and get back to work.

It is time to bust the myth of multitasking. Multitasking is the ability to manage multiple tasks at the same time. Or more accurately, it is the *inability* to manage multiple tasks at the same time. It is the inability to focus on only one thing at a time. It is being distracted and having trouble prioritizing and determining what's important in the moment. It is doing too much simultaneously and failing to recognize the consequences of spreading your resources thin.

Because of the demands of daily life and the capabilities of modern technology, multitasking has become a necessity. Several things require your attention at once, which means multitasking at home, multitasking at work, and multitasking even when you socialize. You could be driving the kids to school while planning a meeting on the phone; talking to a client on the phone while surfing the net for important information; or working on a project at home while talking on the phone, cooking a meal, and listening to music all at the same time.

But although it is considered an efficient way of doing

---

[*] This is not exactly how adult ADHD came about, but the process was very similar.

things, multitasking can easily add hours to your work-
day and years to your goal achievement. You may think
that doing two things at once will cut the time in half. It
doesn't. It actually doubles the time and it doubles the
effort. As a result, it cuts in half the odds of success.

The Confessional

Gene sat behind the wheel of the Ford Crown Victoria se-
dan. He turned on the ignition and pulled out of the
parking spot. He drove toward the on-ramp to the near-
est interstate and set off for his twenty-four-mile journey.
It was a nice day. Lack of precipitation, good visibility,
and light traffic made driving conditions ideal. Gene was
driving in the right lane, at an average speed of sixty-two
miles per hour, keeping a distance of about 150 feet from
the car in front of him, a reasonable distance to give him
enough time to react quickly and appropriately should
he need to slow down. About ten minutes later his cell
phone rang. Being a safe and conscientious driver, Gene
had his hands-free headset already connected to his
phone, so all he had to do was just press Accept and start
talking, without getting distracted. It was his assistant
who called him to talk about a few issues that Gene
needed to discuss.

About fifteen minutes into the conversation Gene
saw brake lights and the car he was following slowing
down significantly. The distance between them was now
much shorter; they were less than a hundred feet apart,
and getting closer. Gene reacted as quickly as he could.

He stepped on the Crown Vic's brakes, but at sixty miles per hour the bulky car wasn't responding swiftly. Within seconds the inevitable happened. Gene rear-ended the car in front of him. At twenty-nine years old, and with eight years of driving experience under his belt, Gene had a clean driving record and considered himself a good driver. A few days earlier, though, he almost got into another accident, while driving under the influence of alcohol. His blood alcohol content was 0.08 percent, which legally means "impaired," or too drunk to drive.

Gene wasn't the only person who got into a minor accident or who was driving drunk. He was joined by thirty-nine more people, who participated in an experiment to test (on a driving simulator) who is a worse driver, someone drunk or someone talking on a cell phone? The researchers discovered that a person driving drunk is likely to make a lot more errors than the same person driving sober under identical conditions. But that's not surprising. What *is* surprising is that when tested again under the same road conditions while talking on a cell phone, the same person was as bad as when driving drunk. There was only one difference between driving drunk and driving while on the phone: The driver was more likely to get into an accident when on the phone, regardless of whether a hands-free or a handheld device was used![1]

Talking on the phone while driving is the best example of multitasking but not the only one. The brainblock of multitasking is pervasive, especially given today's smartphone technology. Many of us start the day by checking our to-do lists on our phones, only to spot a notification informing us that we have new email, or a text message, or a Twitter update, and so on. By the time we have come back to our list, nothing has been checked off. And this could all be happening during a staff meeting.

Spotting the Brainblock

The primary action related to multitasking is *digressing*: intentionally or unintentionally getting off track.

Primary Action:

I digress

What are the signs of multitasking?

1. YOU HAVE EVIDENCE THAT YOU CAN MULTITASK . . .

At work

You can barely go through one hour of work without doing any of the following: check email, send a text, make a phone call, Google something, watch something on YouTube, post something else on Facebook, tweet something else on Twitter, listen to music on Spotify or Pandora, Shazam the song you like, and go to iTunes or Google Play to buy it, and while you are there look for cool apps for your smartphone.

Or even when you socialize

You can also barely go through an hour of dinner conversation with friends without doing any of the above.

Which is why you have so much on your plate

Your life is a curse of competing demands. You are like a waiter or waitress in a restaurant, trying to take as many orders and serve as many customers as possible during your shift. You are constantly juggling multiple tasks. You are required to make multiple decisions. You are expected to complete projects, return calls, pick up people from places, prepare other people to go to other places, maintain a full caseload, a functional household, and your sanity all at the same time. Isn't this proof that you can multitask?

And you are constantly overbooked

Procrastination and impatience make you distort the length of time. You think that time is either endless or running out, respectively. But with multitasking, you distort the depth of time. You try to fit as much as you can in the same amount of time. In the same time slot, you can answer emails, be on a conference call, and double-check your spreadsheets for your next meeting. All of that, while you have NPR playing in the background. Each page on your daily calendar looks like a mini-novel.

2. BUT YOU STARTED NOTICING SOME UNUSUAL SYMPTOMS . . .

You can't stay focused

Multitasking means you can't focus on one thing for too long. After a while you find yourself drifting. You can't concentrate much on a single task, especially if the task is long, tedious, or boring.

You need boosters

Your mind wanders, you start daydreaming, thinking about other things, and eventually you shift your attention from the task at hand to something else. Something more stimulating. You start suspecting you have ADHD. Coffee please! (Or maybe Ritalin?)

You feel too tired too often

Multitasking takes up a lot of energy. Moving from one thing to the next makes you feel overwhelmed and exhausted. You get tired juggling multiple mental and physical tasks and hoping to do a good job at each.

But you wonder whether you do a good job

You make careless and avoidable mistakes. You start and leave things in the middle, and never finish them. You lose things, you lose track, you lose your train of thought. You forget ideas, miss appointments, and fail to reply to emails and phone calls.

And you need to rewind a lot

You don't pay attention to what's going on around you. You often catch yourself wondering "What did they just say?" It's easy to rewind, if you are watching a movie at home while checking email. But if you are attending a business meeting, taking a seminar, or talking to a friend, and checking email at the same time, you won't be able to rewind.

3. AND THE MOST DISTURBING OF SYMPTOMS . . .

There is too much noise in your head
In the middle of a conversation you stop listening and start crafting your answer in your head. Other times you use your inner voice to criticize the other person while he or she is still talking. Even worse, sometimes you are thinking about whether you turned off the iron this morning, instead of focusing on the discussion.

That you can't turn off
The noise in your head from your own thoughts gets too loud and splits your attention. You are no longer fully present. While we think of multitasking when we refer to physical tasks, shifting your attention from what's out there to what's in your head is also causing an attention bottleneck. Your focus shifts back and forth between external and internal stimuli.

Where does all this busyness originate?

Behind the Brainblock:
Failure in Attention Management

BRAINS VS. COMPUTERS

The term *multitasking* was first applied to computers to refer to their capability to execute multiple programs at once. This accomplishment was huge. It created a leap in efficiency. Now all requests could be made at the same time, instead of having to wait for the computer to execute one command after the other. As computers started becoming more and more powerful and Internet connections faster and better, the capability of multitasking on your desktop increased exponentially. You could now watch YouTube videos while reading an Acrobat file, making notes in a Word document, and transferring numbers to an Excel sheet. Computers became great at multitasking. But what about you? Is your biocomputer advanced enough to execute multiple commands at once?

The answer is yes. Your brain is capable of handling multitasking, and in fact, it is exceptionally good at it. Stop reading for a moment and think about what you are doing right now. You are holding a book, reaching for the pages, and flipping them using the right amount of force (or holding an e-reader and swiping the screen in the correct place). You are processing the content, understanding the meaning, creating visual images, and probably making silent comments about what you read. At the same time your heart continues to beat, your body temperature is at a comfortable 98.6°F, and you continue to breathe normally. You are able to notice any sounds or smells around you, and you know if you are alone or with other people. You also know who you are, why you are reading the book, and what you would like to achieve in the next few months.

Your brain does all of that, and much more, simultaneously. Millions of calculations go on in your brain at any given moment. That would be your brain multitasking. Your brain carries out most of these functions automatically. This means that to execute these commands the brain does not need you to consciously direct or supervise. Your brain can quietly keep you warm and safe, while you devote time to more important activities, like reading this book, writing yours, or critiquing someone else's.

There is, however, a caveat to multitasking. While your brain can handle multiple things at once in the background, it can only handle one thing at a time in the foreground. You can be doing several things at once, but you can pay attention to only one of them. There is a limit to how much you can focus on. The rest becomes background. This is very similar to what happens with computers. A lot of processes are working in the background, but you can have only one *active* window at a time. You can either type words in an open document or type a website URL in an open browser, but not both simultaneously. You have only one pointer available, and the pointer needs to rest on a single window. Otherwise, you won't be able to accomplish anything.

In a very similar manner, your brain can focus on only one thing at a time. What you focus on depends on the situation and what you need to pay attention to. When you read a book, you focus on the string of written words on the pages and try to extract their meaning. When you listen to someone speak, you focus on what he says and try to understand it. When you drive, you focus on what's happening on the road in front of you.

The scope of what we can focus on is so narrow that even during simple tasks we can concentrate on only one feature of the situation at a time. For example, if I told you to count the words on this page as you read, how well do you think you would be able to also process the content? Most likely, if you took a quiz at the end, you would fail. Similarly, how much attention do you think you would pay on the road, if you were driving and talking on your cell phone at the same time?*

ATTENTION: THE GREATEST GIFT OF ALL

The primary brain function behind multitasking is attention. Attention is the heightened and momentary conscious awareness of an internal or external stimulus. It is the choosing and processing of the foreground, and ignoring the background. The brain shifts our attention to what it considers important in the moment. The

---

* In 2011, the World Health Organization published a special report that highlighted the increased risk of automobile accidents due to driver distraction. Guess what was the main distractor for drivers? Cell phone use!

importance is determined by the nature of your goal in that situation. When you are driving, you pay attention to the obstacles on the road in front of you. When you are having a meeting with your business team, you are listening to what each team member is saying. When you are watching a baseball game, you are focused on the pitcher–catcher pair.

Imagine that you are in a dark room and all you have is a flashlight. Attention is like the beam of the flashlight. All you can see is what's captured inside the small-diameter beam of light. To see what's in the room you have to move it around, but you can see only where you shine the light. The rest of the room fades in the background. While you can use the flashlight to walk through the room without stumbling on loose objects and falling, you cannot light up the whole room at once.

Scientists have discovered that there are many different ways in which we use our attention to interact with the environment.[2] Most of the research suggests that there are four major types of attention management:

Focusing: Turning on the flashlight. Focusing allows you to perceive what's around you and start choosing where to land your attention. Focusing is just like turning on the flashlight, shining the light in front of you, and starting to notice what's there before you make your way around the dark room. If you don't turn the flashlight on, you will be stuck or you will hurt yourself trying to walk around in the dark. Focusing is knowing what your goal is in the moment.

Sustaining: Keeping the light on and steady. Sustaining your attention means being able to concentrate on something for a long time. It means constantly shining your flashlight in the same direction as you walk through the room, instead of shining on one spot, and then another, and another. If you can't keep the light shining in the same direction, you will get confused about which way to go, wander around the room aimlessly, or stumble on a piece of furniture and fall. Sustaining your attention allows you to engage in tasks related to your goals for as long as necessary without getting bored, tired, or sleepy.

Selecting/ignoring: Keeping the light on one spot. Selecting/ignoring is being able to concentrate on one thing and ignore all other distractions. Selecting/ignoring is when you hold the flashlight in front of you and you make your way through the room determined to get to the other side. But then your phone starts ringing. What do you do? Do you stop to answer it? Or you hear a dog barking outside. Do you go out to see why the dog is barking? If you give in to all the distractions, your flashlight will run out of batteries before you make it halfway through the room. Selecting/ignoring is being able to stick to a task related to your goal and tune out everything else.

Shifting: Moving the light around. This fourth type refers to what you do when there are multiple stimuli that require your attention. What happens when you need to take care of several things at once? How do you handle tasks that need to be done simultaneously? In other words, how do you multitask?

For a long time, scientists believed that there was a type of attention that allowed us to work on two tasks at the same time. This brain function was called divided attention, and it was considered the reason you are able to simultaneously drive and talk on the phone or read the paper and listen to music or take notes and talk during a meeting. Then scientists started noticing that when people were engaged in two tasks at the same time, their performance suffered. They started missing parts of what was going on and making more mistakes on one or both of the tasks. Study after study started showing that maybe divided attention was more of an urban legend than an actual brain ability. Think of the flashlight analogy. You are still holding the same flashlight, with the same beam of light, of the same width and brightness. But now imagine that as you shine the light to find your way to the other end of the dark room, you also need to shine the light on your phone to find your cousin's phone number to call, on the wood floor to look for water damage, and on your hands to make sure you have your wedding band on. How can you make one beam of light illuminate all of these things at once?

You can't. The only way to accomplish something like that would be to do each task one at a time. And that brings us to the other type of attention, the kind that you need when you have more than one thing on your plate. Shifting or alternating attention is being able to switch back and forth from one relevant task to another. It is the ability to stop in the middle of doing something, turn your attention to something else, and then come back to the previous task and pick up where you left off. Shifting is what allows you to answer a call at work while you are in the middle of reviewing a budget proposal, and then get back to the budget after you are done with the phone conversation. It is what allows you to multitask.

Think of divided attention and alternating attention as parallel multitasking and serial multitasking. If the two tasks at hand are cooking and talking on the phone, divided attention would be cooking and using a hands-free device to make the phone call and talk while cooking. Alternating attention would be cooking, taking a break to make a phone call, finish the conversation, and then return to cooking (and hoping that you didn't burn the food!).

Divided attention, or parallel multitasking, means that 100 percent of your attention capacity is split between tasks. For example, one task gets 70 percent and the other gets 30 percent. This means that none of the two tasks gets 100 percent of your attention. The only way you can be efficient and productive with parallel multitasking is when you are engaged in a task that requires some attention and another that you can do almost automatically. Walking casually in the park (automatic) and having a conversation with a friend (serious or casual) is an example of that. Walking in a familiar, relatively quiet place is not a task that requires too much attention, so most of your attention can be devoted to your friend. But when the same conversation happens while you are trying to find your way around in a new town, you are 30 percent in listening mode, 30 percent in reading street signs mode, and 40 percent looking for a map mode. In this case, not only are you missing half of what your friend is saying, but you can't find your way around and you risk running into oncoming traffic.

Alternating attention, or serial multitasking, means that 100 percent of your attention is on one task, then you move 100 percent of your attention to another task, and then 100 percent of your attention back to the original task. You take a clean break from the conversation to check the incoming text messages, respond if you have to, and then continue with the conversation. Serial multitasking sounds easier but it's not. Shifting 100 percent of your attention from task to task to task requires a tremendous amount of energy. You need to mark where you are on task 1, move on to task 2, orient yourself to what you need to do, put task 1 out of mind, focus on task 2, work on it, mark where you are, go back to task 1, refresh your memory, reorient yourself, forget about task 2, and so on and so forth. Not only does all this back and forth make you more tired, but it also makes you more prone to making mistakes.

While shifting allows you to work on multiple things at a time, it is the first three types of attention management that allow you to do any one thing well. Focusing allows you to determine what's important and therefore what you need to concentrate on—should I watch my favorite show on TV or should I finish my presentation for tomorrow? Sustaining makes it possible to focus on something for a long time to process it, understand it, and master it—I will work on my presentation until I get it done and feel comfortable delivering it. Selecting/ignoring prevents you from getting distracted by external or internal interference—I will resist checking my email, I will stop paying attention to the children playing outside, and I will stay away from the freezer where I can hear the ice cream screaming my name.

These are the kinds of skills that should be listed on your competence résumé. Managing your attention well is much more important for achieving your goals than multitasking.

Brainblock Side Effects

Unfortunately, in most cases multitasking is not a skill to brag about, but a bad habit to kick. It weakens your ability to concentrate, to stay focused on something for a long time. But it also makes it hard to know what to pay attention to. You fail to recognize what's important in the moment, what your priority should be, and how to allocate your resources. You are more vulnerable to distractions. Your resistance to the lure of easy and familiar diminishes. Your brain starts following the path of least resistance.

Nothing makes your actions less effective than multitasking. The line between multitasking and floundering is very thin. Giving in to distractions, trying to fit too many items on a small agenda, and jumping around from task to task will take its toll on your ability to achieve your goals.

What are the side effects of multitasking?

A JACK OF ALL TRADES IS A KING OF NONE

For better or for worse, you come equipped with only one flashlight. Your brain is designed in a way that keeps your foreground focus narrow and your background perception broad. Some people may have brighter or wider flashlights than others, but each person comes equipped with only one. This means that you can shine the flashlight in only one direction at a time. When you move the beam in all directions, you will get a sense of what's going on around you, but you won't be able to perceive the fine details of anything.

Multitasking is the enemy of excellence. Juggling too many things at once means fewer resources available for each. Having fewer resources means less attention to detail and a product of lesser quality. When you squeeze multiple tasks into the same time slot, your attention is split, your brain gets tired faster, and the end result is a messier, Swiss cheese–like product. When you squeeze multiple projects into your life, you will often feel overwhelmed, exhausted, rushed, and inefficient.

Multitasking affects how you learn new things, how you apply what you learn, and how well you can teach others. You may become a jack of all trades but you will never be a king of any.

LIVING WITH LOOSE ENDS

Multitasking is like living inside parentheses. You have to keep opening and closing parentheses, until at some point you lose track and you have no idea where to begin and where to end. It feels like trying to solve this equation:

$$(14+(4\times5(6+1-9)))/(6+8(4-(20/10)$$
$$+72/(3\times3)+7+(9-4)/5\times(3+(8/4)/5))))$$
$$= x$$

The more you multitask, the more loose ends you will have to tie. The more loose ends you have to tie, the more of them will remain loose.

When you are working on too many projects at once, staying on top of each is very challenging. Many projects means many tasks with multiple steps to manage and monitor. This is a recipe for disaster. You leave yourself no room for *thinking* time because *doing* time uses up all your resources. Without careful management, you will inevitably skip and forget steps. Tracking your progress becomes a nightmare, and hopes of ever finishing any one project disappear. The end result is a slew of unfinished projects.

MULTITASKING IS MULTITAXING

Multitasking is not fuel-efficient. It requires a lot of energy. Splitting your attention among many tasks is much more wasteful, in terms of brainpower, than focusing on one activity alone. Shifting your attention back and forth from one task to another takes up a significant amount of mental energy. Returning to a task, reorienting, and restarting requires effort, especially if you aim to do a good job. In essence, by skipping around or juggling multiple activities, you are making your brain more tired. This means again that you will peter out sooner, you won't be able to sustain your attention for very long, and you will be more likely to make mistakes, because of mental fatigue. At the end, you will spend more time recovering and restarting than if you had chosen to leave multitasking to computers.

USE IT OR LOSE IT

Losing the ability to stay focused is the most devastating consequence of multitasking. Not only does daily living require multitasking, but it also makes it very inviting. Distractions are everywhere, and they are loud and alluring. All the smart and quick devices that you have in your possession make it so easy to have a vast amount of information at your fingertips. Do you need to find a restaurant? Go on Yelp, read reviews, and then go on OpenTable and make a reservation. Did you stumble on a beautiful sunset? Take a snapshot and post it on Instagram. Do you have a thought that no one cares about but you feel the impulse to share it anyway? Update your Facebook status. With all this power in your hands, dinner conversation seems like the real distraction.

Does that mean we are losing the ability to stay focused on one thing at a time? Will our brains adapt to this frantic pace of living? Is staying focused on something for more than five seconds a skill at risk of extinction? What does this mean for the way we live our lives?

It means children will be unable to sit still in the classroom and pay attention to their teachers. Friends will not be able to have dinner conversation without texting, tweeting, or blogging. Employees will be suffering during long meetings. Churchgoers will be fidgeting through a sermon. And even therapists will have difficulty getting through an hour-long psychotherapy session before their brains explode!

Smashing the Brainblock

To win the battle against multitasking you can keep your plate full, but organize the food in a way that allows you to choose what to eat, and eat one kind at a time.

STRATEGY 1: PRACTICE MONOTASKING

Paolo Cardini introduced a great antidote to multitasking in a TED talk in 2012: monotasking.[3] Now that's a skill worth developing! In a world full of voices calling for your attention, focusing on one and only one is a battle worth winning.

To make the most out of your flashlight, you have to keep shining the light steadily on what's in front of you without moving it all over the place. The same rule applies to the way you approach action in your day-to-day life. To get anything done, and done well, you must stay focused on the task at hand. When you find yourself drifting into another task, remind yourself of your goal in the moment. Ask yourself what you are supposed to be doing right now, answer the question, and monotask away!

Are you cooking? Stay over your kitchen counter, and limit your multitasking to chopping, whipping, broiling, and flipping. Stop texting, calling, watching *American Idol*, and ordering cookbooks from Amazon on your iPad.

Are you driving? Hands on the wheel, eyes on the road, foot on the pedal. No hands on the GPS, no eyes on the incoming text, no feet on the dashboard.

Are you doing research online for a project? Make sure the keywords you use do not include words like *vacation*, *cheap flights*, *shoes*, *used car*, *baseball*, and *best dressed at the Oscars*.

Are you spending time with a friend? Here is what works: making eye contact, listening, nodding, responding, repeating. Do not check email, respond to texts, flirt with the waitress, or be thinking (silently) about work.

An exception to this rule: You are allowed to *sidetask* when necessary. Imagine that you are in the middle of something, like a conversation with someone about one of your projects, and you are struck by an idea related to another one of your projects. Give yourself a very short break and write down the idea. Don't spend *any* time on it at that moment but also do not let it slip away because it will never come back. Sidetasking is like having a little notepad next to you, to put down anything that distracts your attention from the task at hand. Use it wisely and sparsely because it can quickly turn to multitasking.

STRATEGY 2: TRAIN YOUR BRAIN

If you are like most people, you probably have some type of workout routine. You do a little bit of cardio, some push-ups and sit-ups, some weights, and maybe every other Saturday you try yoga. The reason you go through this routine is not because you plan to become a professional runner, weight lifter, or a yogi. You do it because you want to be in good health, avoid injuries and pain, and lift boxes or carry shopping bags more easily.

Your brain needs the same kind of workout as well. There are several training programs nowadays that are available online or as apps that provide a wide range of brain exercises. These exercises are designed to engage brain pathways that control specific cognitive functions, to make them stronger and more efficient. They feel like video games and are stimulating, challenging, and entertaining. The programs keep track of your progress and they challenge you based on your performance. Almost all of these training programs include a variety of attention exercises.

Two programs whose effectiveness is backed up by research include Lumosity (lumosity.com) and BrainHQ from PositScience (brainhq.com). These training programs are helpful in two ways: First, they help you strengthen your attention "muscle." There is evidence that such programs can help improve your cognitive skills, like attention or visual processing. Second, play-

ing the game is in and of itself an exercise in attention. You need to stay focused, and you have to ignore
distractions (some of the games train you to do that). You
cannot be doing the exercise and be doing something
else at the same time. If you don't pay attention, you will
get a bad score, which will haunt you for days on your
scoreboard!

Ideally, the recommendation is to train daily, but doing the exercises as often as you can works as well. Keep
in mind, though, that doing well in these exercises alone
is only one factor in being a peak performer. You must
apply the same kind of disciplined attention to all other
tasks in life to reap the benefits.

STRATEGY 3: FIND YOUR TRAPS

The world is full of traps. Television, computers, smart-
phones, social media, exciting blogs, fancy apps, and
other bright, shiny objects are lurking in the background
to grab your attention and keep it hostage. These great
tech options make multitasking possible and easy. But
don't be fooled. They are there to kidnap your attention,
break it down, and eat it up in small pieces. They make
you think you are multitasking, but they actually keep
you scattered.

One way of preventing yourself from getting trapped
is to know where the traps are. Here is a challenge: Identify your five top distractions. Find the five things that
trap your attention, that shift your focus away from the
main task and toward side tasks. Think about activities
that you usually do together to get more done in less

time, to get more stimulated, or to take a break from work.

Here are the top five traps for most people:

- **Television.** A very treacherous trap, and DVR and streaming capabilities make it worse. At least before that era you knew when the good shows were on, and you could devote Thursday night to watching your favorite sitcoms. Now there is access to anything at any time. Saying that you will put the TV on just for company while getting something else done is a miserable lie. You will fail to resist. Solution? Turn the TV off.

- **Internet.** Never before has it been more convenient to do research while working on a project. As questions come up, you can go to your favorite search engine and find the answers you need. And more answers. And related answers. And unrelated answers. And unrelated research. Before you know it, you are on a different topic altogether. Your focus is gone. Solution? Sidetask. Open the website of interest in a new tab, leave it open for later, and immediately return to the active window or tab. If the new tab contains useful information, it will be available for you to get to it later. If not, after a few days you close that tab and never have to think about it again.

- **Food.** Eating and working is the perfect example of divided attention. You can do both at the same time. Especially when the work is sedentary, mindless, or doesn't require too much speaking or manipulation, chewing while working is a piece of cake (no pun intended). But beware! First, when you do both simultaneously, you eat more than you need and work less than you intended. Second, you associate work with food. As soon as you sit down to do work you crave food. You get both distracted and fatter! Solution? Drink more water. It keeps you full, hydrated, and satisfies your oral needs!

- **Smartphone.** Its shiny, sleek exterior and its dark, mysterious touch screen hiding millions of treasures behind it make you want to hold it, slide it, tap it, and get lost in it. This urge takes over regardless of setting: It happens at a work meeting, at home, in the office, at dinner, in the movie theater, everywhere. Literally, multitasking at your fingertips! Solution? Make it inaccessible. Put it in a deep pocket, zip it up inside your bag, or leave it in a different room, so that reaching it requires extra effort.

- **Meetings.** Being around people, working in teams, and doing things together can be both productive and enjoyable. But there is risk that meetings become an excuse for people to get together and socialize, while pretending they are working on an important project. In the middle of a meeting people shift back and forth from work mode to play mode, getting distracted and not getting much done. Solution? Leave time for "play" at the beginning and end of the meeting and do the work in between.

STRATEGY 4: HAVE FAITH IN YOUR TO-DO LIST

If you do not use a to-do list, stop reading right now, go find a piece of paper, and start creating one from scratch. If you have one that is not working for you, there are several books, blogs, and apps that lay out many different options for to-do lists. My favorite is the Todo app by Appigo. The emphasis is on *favorite*, not *best*. You have to really like the to-do list you use. Otherwise, you won't use it.

Let's do some research. Get hold of your to-do list and check for entries that combine tasks. For example, see if you've written tasks like "call the insurance company and review class notes." Or "work on the grant proposal and plan the committee meeting." Or "read the latest updates on antidepressants and eat cookies." Can you find any? Doubtful. The reason is simple. Multitasking doesn't make sense intuitively. We don't naturally plan to blend tasks. We somehow know that the most effective way to get things done is one at a time, fully focused and free from distractions.

Have your to-do list readily available and get in the habit of checking it often, and especially before you start working on something. Decide which tasks you will pursue in the moment and agree (with yourself) to stick to them. If in the middle of a task you think about something else that needs to get done, then sidetask. Take a few seconds and put that task on your list. Don't stop what you are doing to do something else. Have faith that your to-do list will safeguard it for you to pick up when you are ready.

STRATEGY 5: LEARN TO SAY NO

Your big heart and good intentions are often the reason that you multitask. People come to you for help and you can't resist the temptation to be a good Samaritan. It may be your boss who dumps more work on your desk, a friend who asks you to help her with a project, or the PTA that seduces you into planning an event. You feel obligated to do things for others on top of everything you have to do for yourself. You agree to help out because it's so hard to say no when your help is needed. Many people I know—out of eagerness, responsibility, and desire to give back to their professional community—take on so many more projects than they *know* they can handle. More projects, more deadlines, plus the same amount of time, equals multitasking.

You must, must, must learn to say no. Set aside your feelings of worry about someone else's project and guilt over not being able to help. Budget your energy well and determine how much time you have available to help others, without hurting your own work and without cheating yourself out of time and energy needed for your own projects.

STRATEGY 6: LEARN TO DELEGATE

You have many skills and many talents. You have accomplished a lot in your life, even if you don't always see it or acknowledge it. You put on different hats and juggle multiple tasks. You are creative, you are energetic, and you help others in need. You are a king of your trade.

But you are not a jack of all trades. You are not superhuman. You don't know everything. And you can't do everything on your own. Nor should you. One of the best remedies for multitasking is delegating. Knowing what to delegate is very important. Multitasking can clutter your brain in a way that makes it difficult to decide what to assign someone else and what to do yourself. But delegating can also be stressful. Losing control of an aspect of your work by having someone else do it instead may end up creating more work for you at the end. Someone else may not do the work as well as you would, or require extensive supervision. Or they may agree to do something for you and never follow through. While that's likely to happen and very frustrating when it does, asking someone for help when you don't know how or you don't have time to do it yourself will help you allocate your resources and get better results.

Think of delegating as quid pro quo. How often have you helped someone else who asked for help? Now it's time for them to reciprocate. Of course the most straightforward quid pro quo arrangement is hiring someone to do the work. You pay them money, and therefore help them pay their bills. They do the work, and therefore help you accomplish your goals.

STRATEGY 7: EMBRACE BOREDOM, THE NATURAL BRAIN TRAINER

People are losing their ability to tolerate boredom. Being immersed in an ocean of interesting and exciting possibilities makes it very hard to persist with something boring and uninspiring.

Boredom breeds multitasking. It's hard to be engaged in anything that you find dull, tedious, and unexciting. Such tasks don't grab you. They don't get your attention hooked. Doing something uninteresting doesn't pull you in and doesn't hold you there. First, you start avoiding tasks, putting them off, or rushing them, and then you start combining them with something more exciting (multitasking). You go running with a friend to make it more fun, you drive to work while listening to your audiobooks to make the commute more bearable, and you check your email during a long meeting to stay awake.

Unfortunately, chronic multitasking makes monotasking seem boring. Multitasking makes you feel stimulated and energetic; monotasking makes you numb and bored. But it is the boring tasks that provide the best kind of brain training. Sticking it out with something that seems long and tedious is a great and natural attention workout. Seek out these opportunities and use them as a natural way to expand your attention span.

Identify three situations that normally make you feel bored and fuel your urge to multitask. I, for example, get really bored during meetings in which my role is peripheral, during long conversations on the phone with certain relatives (identities concealed), and waiting on the subway platform for the train to arrive. What are your three?

1. _____

2. _____

3. _____

The next time you are in these situations, practice monotasking. Focus on the boring task for five minutes, and do nothing else during that time. Take a one-minute break (check your phone, eat your power bar, drink some tea), and refocus on the task for another five minutes. Keep repeating, till the activity is completed. The next time, go for ten-minute increments, and each time keep increasing by five-minute increments until you are able to go through the entire thing with as few breaks as possible.

■ ■ ■ ■ ■ ■ ■

RIGIDITY

The Slippery Slope of Persistence

Rigorous or rigid? Determined or stubborn? Single-minded or narrow-minded?

There is a big difference between sticking to your guns and digging in your heels. Following the plan is persistence; refusing to tweak it in response to circumstances is rigidity. Being right is rewarding; believing you are never wrong is being blind.

Rigidity is the barricade to progress. Change is inevitable. People change, circumstances change, and the times change. Rigid people resist change. They do their best to stay the same. They fight tooth and nail to defend their opinions, to uphold their purpose, and to stay the course. And while withstanding the passage of time may be extremely valuable for an heirloom or an antique, it is disastrous for a living organism interacting with a living environment. Many species would have been extinct thousands of years ago had they not been able to adjust to a likewise changing environment. That is the essence of evolution: growth and progress that stems from the ability to detect and adapt to changes.

The same thing that happens to plants and animals happens to people. If they want to remain in control of their fate, people must be able to change. To survive, they must be vigilant to changes in the environment. They must be flexible and adapt quickly to new circumstances. They must continuously generate new ways, new approaches, and new techniques to be able to master a rapidly changing physical, social, and technological world. Those who are the most adaptive, the most agile, and the most versatile are the ones with the highest chances of success. The rigid are the ones most likely to become extinct.

To accomplish a goal you need to take action. When the action you are taking isn't yielding the desired results, there may be something wrong with what you are doing. You need to step back, reassess, identify errors, and change what you do. Rigidity is all about change. Or better, the absence of change. A very popular, but alas misattributed, quote defines insanity as doing the same thing over and over and expecting different results. The quote is often mistakenly attributed to Albert Einstein, which gives it huge credibility, but unfortunately there is no evidence that he is the source of that wise statement.[1] Regardless of who said it first, its essence remains the same: Insanity is using the same approach, applying the same strategies, taking the same action, and expecting different results. Is rigidity a form of insanity?

More important, how do you change the enemy of change?

The Confessional

Robert is an anthropology professor in one of the largest public universities in the country. He and his wife, Linda, who was also on the faculty in the same department, had worked there side by side for almost thirty years. Unlike other couples who have difficulty mixing work and home life, Robert and Linda managed to blend the two really well. While Robert, now eighty years old, continues to work, Linda was forced to retire earlier than expected, because she started having problems getting her work done. She had become forgetful beyond the absentminded professor kind, had difficulty completing projects, was often confused, started missing appointments, and was getting into an unusually high number of minor car accidents. A few months after she retired, Linda was diagnosed with early stage Alzheimer's dementia, which unfortunately is a progressive condition that over time robs a person of their ability to function independently. Robert was well aware of that, and arranged his schedule so that he could spend as much time by Linda's side as he could. And although initially this arrangement was working out, it was not a feasible long-term solution.

With Linda's ability to do things around the house diminishing, the onus to maintain the household fell entirely on Robert. Pretty soon he was exhausted. He became irritable, demanding toward other family members, and distrustful of anyone else. He refused to hire someone to help with housekeeping, let alone a professionally trained aide to help with the requisite medical care. When their children suggested that they hire a day nurse, he told them their suggestion was despicable and sent them on a long guilt trip. He told them that it would be cruel and unkind to let a stranger take care of their mother. Meanwhile, the children felt that Robert was being ungrateful and that any kind or amount of help they would offer was not good enough. Eventually, he caved in and hired an aide for a couple of hours a day during the week. And on weekends, he would be husband, housekeeper, and caregiver all at once.

Not long ago, Robert's only grandson was getting married. The wedding had been planned for months, and relatives from all over the country were going to travel to the East Coast to be there. Linda was in no position to travel, so Robert would go alone. He booked himself on a morning flight going out and an evening flight coming back on the same day. A few days before the wedding, Linda developed a low-grade fever that required no more treatment than some Advil. The doctors reassured Robert that there was nothing wrong, and he shouldn't worry about it. But he did worry. He decided to stay home with his wife instead of going to the wedding and canceled his flight. When his children found out, they were upset that

Robert refused to have the aide stay with their mother for the day. They tried to change his mind, but he was adamant. No one could look after his wife like he could, even for one day.

He didn't go. His grandson was disappointed, his children were exasperated, and he missed out on a precious, once-in-a-lifetime moment. He claims he knew what was best for Linda. Unfortunately, no one asked Linda how she felt. Welcome to the land of the rigid.

Spotting the Brainblock

The primary action related to rigidity is *resisting*. Resisting change, resisting the new, resisting progress.

Primary Action:

I resist

These are the signs of rigidity:

1. YOU HAVE AN INTERESTING RELATIONSHIP WITH CHANGE . . .

You don't necessarily like change
Change doesn't excite you. In fact, it scares the living daylights out of you. When you are confronted with the need to change, you become uncomfortable. Whether it is a major change, like switching jobs, or a minor change,

like cutting your hair, your instinct is to resist. Why do you need to change the way you run your business? Why do you need to change the way you talk to your husband? Why do you need to start using social media? Why do you need more personal development training?

But people don't respond well to that
People want you to change. They think you are stubborn and unyielding. You don't understand why. You simply don't want to change your views, your routines, your opinion of yourself and others, or your expectations from life. Ultimately, you are proud of sticking to your guns.

And when you tried to change it didn't work
You often find yourself bummed out because despite your best efforts you can't seem to change your life in the direction you want to. You work hard, you persevere, you keep trying, but nothing changes. You have exhausted your options and you feel exhausted. You tried everything, but still see no results.

So you decided not to believe in change
Even if you think that change is necessary and beneficial, you don't think that it's always possible. Some things are just the way they are. Some situations are unchangeable. You see no way out, no good options, no future results. You are permanently stuck and can hope only for a miracle. When someone offers a suggestion, you shut it down, because you are sure you have already considered it.

2. YOU THINK YOU HAVE MORE CLARITY
THAN OTHER PEOPLE . . .

You know the difference between right and wrong
You know whether the world is good or bad. You know who is stupid and who is smart. You know who is failing and who is succeeding. In life, you can either be right or wrong. There is no room for nuance.

And you are never wrong
Why? Because you said so. Because you are one of the good ones. Because you care. Because you do what you do out of love. Because you are older and wiser. Because you have multiple degrees. Because being wrong is embarrassing and admitting it humiliating.

While other people are still confused
You don't understand all this wishy-washiness around you. You don't understand why people get stuck in the middle ground. Why they can't answer a question with yes or no. Why they can't decide whether abortion is a crime or a right, homosexuality is a chioce or not, and terrorists are evil or victims of circumstance.

3. YOU ALSO THINK YOU KNOW THE RULES . . .

All of them
You know the rules about everything: what you should be eating, how many hours you should sleep, how often you should have sex, at what age you should get married, when you should have kids, how often you should call your mother, how you should treat your boss, and even

what your goals in life should be. And when no known rule exists, you make one up.

You respect them

Rules exist to be followed. Your life is guided by a set of rules. All your decisions are consistent with them.

And enforce them

You live by the rules, and remind others to live by them as well. You make it your mission to enforce them. And you don't like it when people try to break them.

Therefore, it's never your fault

If you follow the rules, you can't be blamed or criticized. If someone was hurt, offended, or upset by something you did, it's not your fault. You followed the rules. Therefore, no apologies are necessary.

Behind the Brainblock: Failure in Mental Flexibility

THE VERSATILE BRAIN

Rigidity is the failure to recognize that the rules of the game have changed and a different approach is needed if you want to keep winning. The brain function that has been delegated essential for this task is mental flexibility.

Mental flexibility is an aspect of the brain's executive functions. The executive functions are the reason we are able to set, pursue, and achieve our goals. They are in charge of planning, initiating, monitoring, and adjusting our actions. They enable us to generate strategies and solve complex life problems. These are the same functions that, when glitching, cause us to procrastinate. So what exactly does mental flexibility do?

Mental flexibility is your ability to track and change how you think and what you do, in order to achieve your goals. There are two parts to mental flexibility.[2] The first part is *responding to change*. Responding to change, also called reactive flexibility, refers to the ability to modify your actions in response to negative feedback or unwanted results. This means that when you realize what you are doing is not helping you reach your goal, you change your course of action to get the results you want. For example, if you have been trying to organize a charity in your community through your blog, and you realize no one has been signing up, you may want to try something else to mobilize the local citizens.

Reactive mental flexibility is activated when one of two things happen. First, when your original action plan is not working out for you. For example, you thought that the best way to get a promotion at work would be to point out to your boss in a subtle way the weaknesses of the other contenders. You keep doing that, but you notice that other people are getting promoted while you are staying in the same position. Then your reactive flexibility becomes activated and you decide to change your approach. Now, instead of pointing out your coworkers' weaknesses, you start highlighting your own achievements to your boss and wait to see if this new action plan is going to be more effective.

Second, reactive mental flexibility is activated when the circumstances have changed and your original course of action needs to be revised. What you are used to doing no longer works for you because the conditions have changed. For example, you may have discovered that the best way to communicate your ideas to your boss at work is during lunch breaks. But there is a change in administration at your company and your old method is not effective anymore. Your new boss does not take lunch with the employees. Now you have to think of a different way to accomplish this goal. You have to find a new way to approach your boss to discuss and explore new ideas.

This leads us to the second part of mental flexibility, which is *creative thinking*. Creative thinking is also called fluency, divergent thinking, or spontaneous flexibility. Creative thinking refers to the ability to generate ideas that are large in number and broad in scope. This aspect of mental flexibility is what allows us to think outside the box and to deal with the complexity of life. Life problems do not have a "right" or "wrong" answer, like simple arithmetic problems do. They have many solutions, and the more solutions you can come up with, the more successful you will be at solving the problem. Mental flexibility is what makes you a good problem solver.

Here is a simple test of your mental flexibility. Grab a

piece of paper (or your laptop, your phone, your tablet, or whatever instrument or device your prefer—exercise your mental flexibility!). Take a few minutes and name all the uses for a sock.[*]

Now look at your responses. How many uses did you come up with? How similar or different are your examples? How elaborate were your answers? How challenging was the task?

Mental flexibility is important for both your short-term and long-term life goals. It can affect not only simple things, like how you deal with being stuck in traffic or having a slow Internet connection, but also more complicated things, like the way you view yourself, how you judge other people, your communication style, your ability to handle challenges, how optimistic you are about the future, how much stress you experience, and even how well you can recover from emotional trauma.

So what happens when this function malfunctions? Rigidity happens.

Rigidity is the result of a brain glitch that shuts down mental flexibility and creates mental rigidity. Mental rigidity is the flipside of flexibility. It is the inability to change what you do or how you think in response to changes in circumstances. In other words, you continue doing the same thing or thinking the same way, even though the circumstances have changed, and what you do is no longer adaptive. You are no longer reacting to

---

[*] Inspired by Guilford's (1967) Alternate Uses Task, a test used to assess creativity.

change, and your creative thinking and problem solving abilities shut down. But you don't see that. Instead, you may think you are doing the right thing and refuse to change. You don't realize that the rules have changed. You persist because you don't see a better or different way of doing things. You get stuck in your old ways. You keep beating a dead horse.

Brainblock Side Effects

Without mental flexibility, people become stubborn. They can't change perspective, their thinking becomes stiff, and they appear unimaginative and unoriginal. But without change, progress is impossible. Resistance to change is the surest way to be stuck in the same place in life, having the same conversations, making the same promises, and feeling the same disappointments.

The rigid are the masters of resistance. But they pay a high price for their self-imposed stability.

NOTHING HAPPENS TO THE RIGID

Of all the brainblocks, rigidity holds the largest share of responsibility for being stuck. Getting unstuck requires changing something, and rigidity is the enemy of change.

Rigidity is a unique kind of developmental arrest. You resist change without realizing that you are actually preventing progress. You strive to remain the same person, but you complain your life is stagnant. Your work situation doesn't change, the numbers on your bank account don't change, the quality of your relationships doesn't change, and the content of your conversations doesn't change. But you persist in your old ways.

You avoid challenging the status quo. Without challenge, however, there is no growth. Challenge is the fertilizer that nourishes the body, the mind, and the spirit. Challenge promotes learning, and without new learning, the body weakens, the mind slows down, and the spirit becomes dispirited.

EXHAUSTION WITHOUT MOTION

Rigid people are not lazy. They are hardworking. They are not afraid of exerting effort. They are just unable to generate forward motion. Rigidity makes you spin your wheels. You put your energy toward preserving old ideas, maintaining the status quo, and repeating the same patterns, none of which has served you well. As a result, nothing in your life changes despite your efforts. Life becomes an endless marathon that takes place on a treadmill. No matter how long or how fast you run on the treadmill, you won't move forward. You are always on the same spot. The race exhausts you without getting you anywhere.

STUCK IN THE BOX, FOR ETERNITY

Rigidity trumps creativity. Unwillingness to explore new ways of thinking and acting leaves you with nothing but the familiar, the overused, or the obsolete. What used to work works no more. What seemed exciting now feels repetitive.

Rigidity kills innovation. Ideas die if they are not refreshed and enriched. Resisting the new, the unfamiliar, the different, the unexplored keeps you stuck inside the box, and keeps the many opportunities waiting for you outside the box obscured from your view.

Whether it affects your career or your love life, parenting skills or cooking skills, eating habits or workout habits, rigidity will leave you at your wit's end. No other block makes you feel stuck in life the same way rigidity does.

STUCK ON SELF-STICKING LABELS

Rigidity makes you have strong opinions about yourself. You label yourself in various ways—by your profession, by your looks, by your bank account, by your flaws, by your marital status, even by your zodiac. I'm fat. I'm picky. I'm poor. I'm shy. I'm too forgiving. I'm too lazy. I'm clinically depressed. Then you feel obligated to be truthful to that label, and you begin to act accordingly. Once the label is attached, you can't take it off. You become affixed to that version of yourself.

Deep down, you think of removing your label as a compromise, as selling out, as betraying who you really are. You end up creating your own stereotype of yourself. This strong attachment to your own label works like a boomerang. You pass up opportunities, you avoid taking chances, you don't try new things, and you never get to shatter your own limits because you want to be consistent with who you think you are. You will defend your label at the expense of your progress.

OFF THE GUEST LIST

It's not fun to work with rigid people. They can drive you crazy. Negotiating with them is like walking on hot coals, but without the enthusiastic cheering of Tony Robbins. It is painful. They are naysayers and idea blockers. Among the nine types of people that Jeff Haden, an author who writes for *Inc.* magazine, suggested you should remove from your inner circle are the *roadblock prophets*, a hybrid version of the rigid.[3] The roadblock prophets will shut down your ideas and won't let you try out new ways.

Rigid people are bad company because they arrive with tunnel vision, they impose their out-of-thin-air rules, they violate the principles of dialogue, and they turn brainstorming into an endless drought.

If you are in a service profession, you know very well that the rigid are the most challenging type of client. They complain endlessly about having tried *everything* and having found *nothing* that works for them. But they will rebuke even the slightest suggestion to try something different. What they are saying in essence is, Why can't you help me change without me actually changing?

But it doesn't stop with rigid clients. Rigid service professionals drive customers crazy. Rigid bosses demoralize their employees. Rigid teachers deprive their students of valuable learning. Rigid doctors make their patients sicker. Rigid husbands, well, unless they change, they risk becoming ex-husbands.

FIGHTING FOR THE WRONG CAUSE

Imagine waking up one day, only to realize that you have been pursuing the wrong goal. All the effort you have put forth has not really taken you where you wanted to be in life. What do you do? The healthy thing to do is to cut your losses, regroup, hold on to what you've learned in the process, and recalibrate your course.

The rigid don't do that. In fact, they would be lucky if they even realized that they have been fighting the wrong battle. Blinded as they are, they are not able to step back and look at the big picture. They fail to realize that persisting on pursuing the same goal the same way is not bringing them what they want. They keep their blinders on and keep moving in the wrong direction, wasting time and energy for the wrong cause.

NEVER LETTING GO

The rigid can't let go. Because they are very strongly attached to their judgments and opinions, they don't let others off the hook easily. Their first impressions turn into lasting impressions, whether justified or not. Once they stick a label on you, you are placed on that shelf permanently. Trying to convince them that what they saw was only a sliver of who you really are or that they saw what might have been a moment of weakness or that you had good reason to do something with which they disagree is an exercise in futility. And if you wronged them somehow, expect no forgiveness. Of course this is not really your problem. They are the ones who choose to hold on to a grudge and never let it go. Feeling chronically resentful makes them suffer more than it bothers anybody else.

Smashing the Brainblock

Defeating rigidity takes time and, most important, an *open* mind. But when you get it under control, your life will be transformed. You will be free from a huge responsibility: having to defend that which doesn't serve you anymore.

STRATEGY 1: LISTEN WITHOUT PREJUDICE

Rigidity is impermeable to feedback. But sometimes you need a fresh perspective, a new angle, or a different point of view. You are surrounded by people who are not only interested in your well-being but also affected by your actions. Any one of them could be a mirror in which you can see your own reflection. Family, friends, teachers, colleagues, supervisors, coaches, therapists, physicians, and many others could be available to you to ask for feedback. Granted, they see you through their own lens, and therefore the image may be distorted, but it's good for you to know what perception they are getting.

Asking for feedback takes courage because it requires you to come face to face with your weaknesses and make

yourself vulnerable to other people, who may intention-
ally or inadvertently hurt you with their comments. To
maximize the benefits of feedback, there are two things
you can do: Be open and find the right people.

a. **Be open.** About two years ago, I was at a conference
and had just finished delivering a presentation to
about a hundred attendees. At the end of the presentation, one of my (rather critical) colleagues and
copresenters pulled me aside and said in a serious
tone: *I have some feedback.* I was startled. My defense
system was instantly activated. I didn't need feedback, and I certainly didn't need it from him. He was
a horrible presenter. Besides, I had literally just
stepped down from the podium, and I wanted to bask
in my glory, not stew in his negativity.

There was no way I could avoid this awkward situation, so I had to pretend I was interested in what he
had to say. His main critique was that I kept repeating my point over and over. I simply smiled and ig-
nored him. I chose to close my ears, dismiss the
comments, refuse to process, and stay annoyed for
the next hour. What a missed learning opportunity.
Days later, I thought about what he said, and I knew
exactly what he meant and why he said it. And I
agreed. But I never told him that.

You don't always hear what you want to hear. Sometimes feedback comes across as criticism. Other
times it comes out of the blue (you didn't ask for it) or
out of left field (it doesn't make sense). Regardless

of how harsh, useless, or off the mark the feedback sounds to you, be open to it. Hear it. Process it. And then decide how you want to use it. Listen to others without prejudice. Don't let rigidity cover your ears. Whether you agree with others or not, appreciate their vantage point. There is something to be learned from everyone. Do not become defensive, because when you close up, you run the risk of missing out on valuable information. Do not discard feedback, even if you don't find it useful right away. Store it and think about it later. Challenge yourself by asking not whether you like the feedback but what you can learn from the feedback.

b. **Find the right people.** Finding people in your life whose feedback you trust is one of the most important gifts you can give yourself. Most people shy away from giving you feedback for fear of hurting you or offending you. Others will shower you with compliments, which may or may not be true. There are people, however, who are excellent at giving constructive feedback. They are good observers, careful listeners, and thorough thinkers. They can easily identify strengths, and they are exceptional at pointing out weaknesses with kindness and candor. But they don't stop there. They make helpful suggestions about how to turn the weaknesses around. So not only do you get a good review, but you also gain guidance and direction, which can help you grow.

To get started, identify three important life tasks that you would like to complete, improve on, or master. They could be managing work-related tasks, achieving a personal goal, changing a character trait, making an important decision, buying a home, finding a hobby, or kicking a bad habit. Now think of three people (one for each area) whose opinions you would really like to hear and whose feedback would be really valuable to you. Make sure you choose people who can tell you things that are helpful, not just things that you like to hear.

Area 1. _____

Person 1. _____

Area 2. _____

Person 2. _____

Area 3. _____

Person 3. _____

If you know the person already, reach out to him and seek his feedback. If you don't know the person, think of different ways to access his wisdom. It could be through reading what he wrote, following him on social media, or connecting with other people that he may know.

STRATEGY 2: PERSEVERE WITHOUT PERSEVERATING

There are two verbs in the English language that sound very similar. The first one is *persevere*. Persevere means to continue pursuing something despite the difficulties, opposition, or discouragement you encounter. The other word is *perseverate*. In neuropsychology, perseverate means to keep doing the same thing, even after the original conditions have changed.

The two words are cognates. They come from the same root, the Latin word *perseverare*, which means "to abide by strictly." And even though they sound very similar, they are vastly different. When you persevere, you persist steadily toward accomplishing a certain goal, despite the obstacles you may encounter. Persevering is what pushes you through challenges and keeps you focused on your goals. Perseverance is characteristic of confident and successful people. Perseverance protects you from giving up.

Perseveration, on the other hand, is perverse perseverance. It means persisting in doing the same thing, even when the situation requires changing your course of action. Perseverating is not a strength. It is rigidity on steroids. It makes you unable to adapt to the new rules of the game. Instead, you insist on playing by the old rules, without realizing your losses. Perseverating is wearing your heavy jacket because technically it's still winter, even though it is 65°F outside. Perseverating is continuing to brood and complain about someone who harmed you, even after you got an apology and made amends.

There is a fine line between persevering and perseverating, which you need to make sure not to cross.

Persisting is *persevering* when you:

- Have a clearly defined, multidimensional goal.
- Have a well-articulated, flexible plan.
- Apply proven strategies.
- Monitor your progress in a systematic way.
- Evaluate interim outcomes to determine the effectiveness of your actions.
- Identify and examine mistakes and failures carefully.
- Engage in problem solving to generate new approaches.
- Seek constructive, helpful feedback and decide how to use it.
- Make adjustments to your plan based on failures, problem solving, and feedback.
- Pursue the same goal, but with a slightly changed approach.

Persisting is *perseverating* when you:

- Have a narrowly focused goal.
- Have a rigid plan.
- Monitor success and failure as opposed to progress.
- Wait till the end to evaluate final outcomes only.
- Treat failures as setbacks to be defeated instead of opportunities to learn from.
- Spend more time complaining than problem solving.
- Seek supportive, sympathetic feedback, for comfort and validation.
- Fail to make adjustments to the plan.
- Pride yourself for not giving up, but . . .
- Pursue the same goal, with the same exact approach.

STRATEGY 3: BRAINSTORM WITH A MISSION

The statement that follows is one of the most important messages in this book: *Every problem has at least three solutions.* They are just waiting for you to discover them. Whenever you feel stuck and out of options, I want you to remember this statement.

Rigidity and creativity are polar opposites. The rigid cannot see past what they already know and have tried. They see no options, no solutions, no way out. This perception, however, is an illusion because there are always options. And your goal should be to find at least three of them!

The best antidote to jolt your creativity and discover the three solutions is brainstorming. Brainstorming is very easy, as long as you do it the right way. There are two important rules to follow when you brainstorm. First, free-associate. Say or write as many ideas as you can. Include anything that comes to mind, without second-guessing or reprocessing. Second, don't judge. In brainstorming, there are no right or wrong answers. So refrain from being an editor or critic and act like a transcriber instead: You do not get to choose what gets included in the transcript.

Let's try it. Think of something you consider to be a problem in your life right now. It could be a decision you need to make, a situation you are stuck in, an event that has upset you emotionally, or anything else that you need to deal with and take action. Write it down. Then start brainstorming: Write down as many possible courses of action as you can think of. Follow the two rules: Free-associate and don't judge. How many ways of solving the problem can you come up with?

If you cannot come up with at least three solutions to each problem you have to handle, you have not brain-stormed hard enough. Don't give up. Continue to gener-ate ideas until you find at least three. Even if you don't think they are the perfect ones (be careful not to get brainblocked by perfectionism, coming up next!), they are still options that are available to you and they are better than thinking "*nothing* works" or "there is *nothing* I can do!"

STRATEGY 4: CHANGE YOUR ROUTINE ON PURPOSE

Sometimes you have to change it up just for the sake of it. Creating change in your routines and habits intention-ally is an unquestionable way to train your brain for change.

When you change circumstances on purpose, you train your brain to find new ways to adapt. Consider for a moment how you run your daily life. You probably have many routines set up, things like showering, commuting, eating lunch, that you do the same way every day, from the minute you wake up to the minute you go to bed. You know these routines so well you don't even have to think before you run them.

Pick one of your routines and break it apart. Find ways to change it, to do something differently. The first time you practice your new routine it may be clunky, clumsy, or klutzy, but with practice you will become more graceful and more efficient. After you master that routine, turn the tables again. The main purpose of doing that is not to develop a bunch of new routines but to master the ability to adapt to new circumstances and learn new routines faster.

There are some daily routines that can be changed very easily: Change what you eat for breakfast, change the way you go to work, change the art on your wall, change your workout schedule. Find one routine that you can change and start with that. It may be easy or challenging, but learning to do the same thing differently gives you tremendous flexibility and multiple paths to accomplishing the same goal.

STRATEGY 5: DON'T BE THE KNOW-IT-ALL; BE THE I-WANT-TO-LEARN-MORE

A famous adage often attributed to Socrates, the Greek philosopher, states: "All I know is that I know nothing." And the man seemed to know a lot. Rigid people, on the other hand, are know-it-alls. They think they know all there is to know. Limited mental flexibility makes it difficult to recognize knowledge gaps and deficits.

There are two problems with being a know-it-all. First, when you believe that you know it all—and you may genuinely believe that you indeed know it all, that you have seen it all, and you have tried it all—you stop learning. If you know it all, you won't learn more.

Second, if you claim you know it all, other people won't feel the need to share their knowledge with you. They may even avoid offering any input, because you are

most likely going to tell them that you already know that
or that they are wrong, because you know better.

An effective strategy to reverse the tendency of
knowing it all is to treat each encounter, each situation,
and each conversation as an opportunity to learn more.
Something that distinguishes experts from semiex-
perts and wannabes is that true experts know what they
don't know. Here is a challenge for you:

STEP 1. Pick an area in which you consider yourself an expert, something about which you consider yourself very
knowledgeable or very skilled.

STEP 2. Identify three gaps in your knowledge that you
would like to fill. Formulate questions you would like to
find answers to (if it is information you want to gain) or
pick three techniques you would like to master (if it is a
skill that you want to develop further).

STEP 3. Take action. Find the answers to your questions
or start practicing the new techniques.

STEP 4. Repeat in six months.

STRATEGY 6: PEEL OFF THE LABEL

How would you describe yourself? Extroverted? Shy? Ar-
tistic? Athletic? Natural leader? Sarcastic? Outdoorsy?
Successful? Complicated? Lazy? Determined? Loving?
Bad negotiator? Good Samaritan?

You can use hundreds of words to describe yourself.
The problem is that at some point these words become

more than just words. They become part of your identity. And after a while they start dictating who you are, what you stand for, and how you will be remembered. They start guiding your choices, your principles, your actions, your relationships, and your legacy. They become firmly affixed *labels* that mark who you are. And rigidity is the glue that holds these labels in place.

Labels put limits on you. They become obstacles to change. You start thinking and acting in ways consistent with your label. Being inconsistent with your label feels like an act of betrayal. You feel like you are not being true to yourself, you are not the real you. Those who know you by that label will be disappointed and may even ostracize you.

When Carol was younger, she couldn't see herself as an athlete. She wasn't naturally good at sports, so not only did she refuse to join any of the sports teams in high school, but she staved off any kind of exercise. She wasn't the athletic type. She affixed that label and let herself and others use it to describe her relationship with physical activity. Things changed when she went to college. There she realized how limiting her view of herself as *not athletic* had been. Quickly she picked up running, swimming, and even aerobics. And she was a pretty strong athlete! Now she can't imagine herself not being physically active. Who knows? If she had started earlier, maybe she could have been an Olympian.

Holding on to a label, especially when the label has no functional value but only sentimental value, is being rigid. It is counterproductive and in many cases deprives you of opportunities to gain new insights and experiences.

How do you remove a label?

STEP 1. Find the labels you have attached to yourself. What are the terms or phrases that you (or others) very commonly use to describe yourself?

STEP 2. Consider all the ways in which these labels are limiting you. What are some things you would do differently, or even do at all, if it weren't for the label?

STEP 3. Define the labels. For instance, when you say something like *I am not athletic*, what do you mean? Do you mean I do not have the body of an athlete? I do not exercise? I do not like to exercise? I do not participate in competitive sports? I don't belong to a local sports team?

STEP 4. Replace the label. Look for two things in your definition: what is essential and what is changeable. *Essential* means that really important aspect of who you are that you could not live without. *Changeable* means that you can change the way you do something or think about something. To the extent you can, save the essential. In Carol's case, she would say "I like to exercise, it is essential to me. Competing is not. What I do to exercise and how often are changeable." If her definition of a non-athlete was "I have not exercised in years," she can't change what happened in the past, and she will be stuck with that label. But she can change what to do from this day on. Now, instead of describing herself as *not the ath-*

letic type, she can say: "Even though I didn't exercise much as a teenager, I like exercising, and exercise is part of my life now." Which statement is more likely to make her exercise more?

Peeling off the label is not betrayal. It is an act of kindness to yourself. It gives you the flexibility to do whatever you like, and still be the person you want to be.

STRATEGY 7: BE YOUR OWN DEVIL'S ADVOCATE

There is no better way of improving your mental flexibility than being your own devil's advocate. Building your argument and then coming up with the counterargument not only makes you great at the art of debate but makes your mind nimble and strong, like a dancer's body. It is a practice that all scientists learn and use. Our entire system of gathering empirical knowledge is based on proving ourselves wrong. That is the purpose of hypothesis testing.

Rigidity results in relentlessly arguing the same point on a topic. Sticking to your point of view prevents you from seeing things from a different angle. Shifting perspectives, however, doesn't necessarily mean that you have to abandon your original point of view. It could also mean that you can identify the weaknesses in your thinking and therefore strengthen your original argument.

Learn to be your own devil's advocate. Challenge your own ideas and beliefs intentionally. Train yourself to see both sides of the coin and to switch back and forth without attachment.

To become a devil's advocate, pick a topic and do a pro and con analysis.

STEP 1. Pick a topic that you have strong feelings about. It could be a decision you made recently, your reaction to something you heard or read, or a belief you hold. Write it down.

STEP 2. Create a table with two columns. Label one of them "Pros" and the other "Cons."

STEP 3. In the Pros column, write down your pros. Pros are the arguments, facts, or ideas supporting your position. What are the advantages of doing things a certain way? What good outcomes are related to this approach? How is it going to benefit you or anyone else involved? Generate as many as possible.

STEP 4. In the Cons column, write down your cons. Cons are the arguments against the position. What are the disadvantages of pursuing this course of action? Can you recall or predict the negative outcomes associated with this position? Generate as many as possible.

STEP 5. Look at the list of Pros and the list of Cons. Are they balanced? Do they include an approximately equal number of entries? A good Pro and Con analysis should make it difficult to decide at a glance whether you should stick to your position or abandon it.

If your pros outnumber your cons by a lot, you still remain rigid!

To close the chapter on rigidity, here is another famous misquote, attributed to Darwin this time: It is not the strongest of the species that survives, nor the most intelligent that survives. It is the one that is most adaptable to change.*

---

* For a discussion about who truly made this statement, check out Nick Matzke's blog, "Panda's Thumb," at pandasthumb.org/archives/2009/09/ survival-of-the-1.html.

PERFECTIONISM

The Quest for the Never Good Enough

Of all the brainblocks, perfectionism sounds the least like a problem. Aiming for perfection implies striving for something desirable and sublime. Perfect. Ideal. Flawless. Free from defects. Having all the desirable characteristics. Made of the best ingredients. Meeting the highest standards. The perfect marriage. The perfect job. The perfect house. The perfect school district. The perfect car. The perfect friends. The perfect answer. The perfect height/weight ratio. The perfect book. Who is willing to settle for less? Who *doesn't* want to excel?

Striving for perfection means setting high standards for yourself, upping your game, raising the bar, meeting the challenge, and exceeding expectations. Perfectionism is the desire and the self-imposed expectation to achieve the highest level of performance.

Then what is the problem with wanting to be perfect? Why is perfectionism a block to goal achievement?

First, *perfect* is undefinable. The "highest level of performance" is hard to define and to measure. The goal of the perfectionist remains elusive, abstract, and a moving target. For perfectionists, nothing less than perfect is acceptable. If something doesn't meet criteria for perfection, it should be discarded, replaced, or redone. But that means that the work of the perfectionist has no end. Things can always be tweaked, changed, and improved— and still not be perfect because *perfect* remains an unknown. For example, every time I look at this paragraph, I find ways to make it sound better. I find better words, I rearrange the sentences to improve the flow, and I include new examples and metaphors. I will keep doing that until it is perfect (that is, I will never stop!). Perfectionism becomes a wild-goose chase.

Second, *perfect* is relative. What is perfect now is not perfect later, and what is perfect for some is not perfect for others. A warm sunny day is perfect for having a picnic but bad if you need rain for your crop. A glass of wine may be the perfect way to end a long day, but not if you are grappling with alcoholism. Salt may be perfect for dressing up a pretzel but not for managing your hypertension. This means that even if perfectionists cover all their bases and create something perfect for everyone, the circumstances may change, and that perfect creation will no longer be perfect for anyone.

The Confessional

After many years of being single, Marcus met someone. He had been dating casually for a while, sometimes going beyond first base, but nothing was serious enough to stick. Although he wasn't too worried, he was in his late thirties and he was ready to find the right one. But none of the women he had been dating made the cut. One was too fat; the other was too thin. One had a weird laughter; the other was still living with her parents. And then there was the one who hadn't been able to find work in two years. One after the other, these women had been rejected for reasons that seemed to make perfect sense only to Marcus.

Marcus came from a prominent family in his relatively small community. He went to very good schools, spoke several languages, and was a good athlete. A serious problem with his health had left him unable to work for many years, but he was slowly regaining his stamina and his confidence and was beginning to explore his career prospects. His family had been very supportive to him throughout the years.

When he first met Nadya, the new girl, Marcus wasn't interested at all romantically, but they started hanging out a lot as friends. After a couple of months, things between them progressed unexpectedly, and before they knew it, they had become romantic. And that's when the real problems started for Marcus. Instead of enjoying this new relationship, he became extremely distressed. He started questioning his decision to be with her. She wasn't as cute as other girls he had dated, she had gone to a state college, she was a little older than he was, and people looked at them weird when they were together. Marcus hadn't introduced Nadya to his friends yet, and he barely told his family about her. What was even stranger was that being alone with her was usually great, and he was enjoying the time they spent together very much. But when they were apart, his mental agony would begin. He was getting physically sick over this affair.

Insight hit him much later. Marcus wasn't single because he hadn't met the right woman. He was single because he didn't want to make a mistake and choose the wrong one. He was single because he couldn't tolerate the idea that his family and friends would think less of him for dating the wrong girl. He was single because he didn't really know what the right girl was like, but insisted on finding her.

Marcus had to work hard to overcome his perfectionism. Lucky for him, Nadya is still around. But she has no idea that he almost had a nervous breakdown deciding what to do. Let's keep that between us!

Spotting the Brainblock

The primary action associated with perfectionism is *obsessing*. Focusing on details, polishing and shining, and never feeling good enough.

Primary Action:

I obsess

These are the major symptoms of perfectionism:

1. YOU AIM HIGH . . .

You don't go for the low-hanging fruit

You set high standards and demand excellence in everything you do. Anything less than Guinness World Record performance is unacceptable. Good is the baseline. Better is where you are. Best is where you want to be. You are not happy with good-enough results. The results need to be outstanding. You have to bake the best cake, write the best book, own the best home, and raise the best child. Only then will you feel settled.

But you often second-guess your achievements

You are never sure whether you've accomplished enough. You always question whether you have done the best you can. You revisit your choices, doubt your decisions, and minimize your achievements. You can always find flaws. Things are rarely very good, and never just right. There is always something to fix, to change, to add, to improve in every aspect of your life.

2. YOU PUNISH YOURSELF . . .

You are haunted by your mistakes

When you achieve your goals, you are beyond ecstatic. But the celebration lasts only until you discover a flaw. Then you start obsessing and ruminating. You start losing sleep over it. You bombard yourself with questions like, How did I let this happen? Why didn't I handle it better? Why couldn't I think of something better or smarter to say? What if I made the wrong decision?

You worry about what others think

You want to make a good impression. Doing something well is not just about challenge and growth but also about validation and approval. You know that others expect a lot of you and you don't want to disappoint them. You feel guilty and ashamed when you think you have let them down. People judge. And if they discover your shortcomings, you will be criticized, ridiculed, and ostracized. Unless you deliver perfection, you expect rejection. You put a lot of pressure on yourself to please all the imaginary judges.

3. OR PUNISH OTHERS . . .

You become the judge

As a perfectionist, you cannot live and let live. Not only do you apply high standards to yourself but you expect other people to be flawless as well. You judge others as harshly as you judge yourself. You are strict, but at least you are not a hypocrite. You don't have double standards—just standards that are twice as high for everyone.

4. YOU ARE THOROUGH . . .

You like law and order
You can't live without order. You spend hours alphabetizing, color coding, aligning, rearranging, straightening, dusting, and disinfecting. When you are done, you wash your hands with soap and water for the recommended fifteen seconds, to make sure you kill every nasty micro-organism on your hands. Your closet is organized by color and fabric, so you can pick the right shirt in the dark. Your home looks more like a West Elm showroom than a place where a real person lives. Your workspace organization puts the staff at the Container Store to shame. You spend a lot of time creating order and even more time maintaining it. If something is out of order, you are out of order too.

You are the embodiment of overthinking
You spend enormous amounts of time defining, analyzing, revisiting, explicating, fine-tuning, and splitting hairs.

You love detail
You check, double-check, and triple-check your work to let no mistake slip through the cracks. You live in the universe of details. You notice things that other people don't. In fact, you notice things that other people couldn't care less about.

But you end up missing the main point

Sometimes you are so focused on the trees that you miss entire forests. Perfectionism is the perfect way to get distracted from the main point. Making something perfect becomes your end goal, and you often miss the target in terms of your initial intention. You focus your efforts on perfecting minor aspects and addressing details and forget the real reason why you are doing something to begin with. For example, the reason for exercising is to have a healthy body, live longer, have more stamina, and feel less pain. It is not to have the perfect body or to find the perfect mate.

Behind the Brainblock: Failure to Prioritize

BREAKING DOWN PERFECTIONISM

Perfectionism is widespread. And not only is it widespread but most people love to claim it. They proudly call themselves perfectionists. In fact, they even assume that in order to be taken seriously they must declare that they have very high standards and are dedicated to reaching them. For example, research shows that when students want to be perceived more positively by their peers and their professors, they are more likely to say that they are perfectionists.[1]

The literature on perfectionism distinguishes two types of perfectionists: the normal or positive perfectionists and the neurotic or negative perfectionists. Positive perfectionists strive for achievement. They invest their energy in setting goals, defeating obstacles, and solving problems. They engage in challenges because doing so gives them pleasure and meaning. They rejoice in achieving their goals. And they seem to be the ones least troubled by the plights that come with perfectionism. In other words, positive perfectionists are psychologically healthy and emotionally stable.

Then there is the dark side of perfectionism. The neurotic or negative perfectionists are the ones who suffer the most. To quote a line from a study comparing positive and negative perfectionism, the goal of a neurotic perfectionist is "to escape mediocrity."[2] Neurotic perfectionists are running away from failure. It is their fear of failing and being exposed that keeps them motivated to perfect their work, not the innate desire to create something magnificent that will give their lives meaning and bliss. Perfection is unattainable for both the positive and the negative perfectionists. But positive perfectionists focus on achievement and negative perfectionists on fear of failure.[3] When their goals are not reached, negative perfectionists are hit hard. They are slow to recover when they run into setbacks, and they are more likely to suffer from low self-esteem, anxiety, and depression.

Having overcome the brainblock of rigidity, I don't believe much in black-and-white distinctions. My opinion is that we all have a little bit of a positive and a little bit of a negative perfectionist in us. Wanting to get things done and do them well is not unique to perfectionists. It is a natural propensity we all have. The desire to create a valuable product, to provide a good service, to achieve high performance, and to maintain good relations is not a brainblock. It is healthy aspiration. In other words, we all have a healthy dose of positive perfectionism. But while our positive perfectionism moves us forward, our negative perfectionism holds us back. What creates the difference? What determines whether we think, feel, and act as positive or negative perfectionists?

SELF-REGULATION: PUTTING FIRST THINGS FIRST

Our ability to achieve goals relies on the effective collaboration between our brain's frontal lobes, where the executive functions and the attention networks are located, and the emotional control centers, which are buried underneath the cortex, the outer and newer layer of the brain. This symphony of brain activity is called self-regulation and is what helps us achieve self-control. Self-regulation determines where we shift our focus, what actions to take, and how to manage our emotions. Self-regulation is how we prioritize our goals and decide what to focus on and what to ignore.

Older theories claimed that the reason people fail to achieve their goals is because they do not apply self-regulation. Newer theories, however, point out that the problem is not always failure in self-regulation. The problem is applying self-regulation toward the wrong goal. And that is the glitch that causes the switch from positive to negative perfectionism. The type of perfectionism we engage in is determined by which goals our brains prioritize.

WHAT FLAVOR IS YOUR GOAL?

Our brain is hardwired to set and achieve goals. But not all goals are created equal. There are goals that move us toward something and goals that move us away from something.

This biologically based feature of goals determines whether we focus on attaining a positive outcome or avoiding a negative outcome. Goals formulated to attain positive outcomes are promotion goals, whereas goals formulated to avert negative outcomes are prevention goals.[4]

Promotion goals involve the pursuit or maintenance of positive outcomes. They are goals about the things we want to accomplish. They refer to states that we strive to maintain or achieve. Examples of promotion goals are getting a higher-paying job, getting a master's degree, looking for a life mate, and planning a vacation to a tropical destination.

Promotion goals are easy to specify and to set timelines for. The final outcome is predetermined and recognizable. Pursuing and achieving a promotion goal results in excitement, eagerness, and elation, whereas failing to achieve it leads to frustration.[5]

In contrast, prevention goals involve the evasion or

relinquishing of negative outcomes. These are goals about the things we want to steer clear of. They refer to states that we strive to change or avoid. Examples of prevention goals are working hard to avoid getting fired, giving in to peer pressure to avoid being ostracized, and going through frequent and unnecessary preventative medical checkups to protect against potentially undiagnosed and untreated health problems.

Prevention goals are more challenging to achieve because their achievement depends on avoiding a negative outcome—that is, running away from something that is not here yet. This means that pursuit of a prevention goal is a never-ending process because the risk of experiencing the negative outcome you want to avoid will always be imminent. For example, if your goal is to avoid getting fired, you have to continue working on that goal until you get fired or retire. Compare that to a promotion goal, like getting a higher-paying job. Once you get that job, your work (on that goal at least) is done.

Pursuing and achieving (to the degree it can be achieved) a prevention goal is associated with feelings of relief and contentment, while failing to achieve is associated with fear, anxiety, and guilt. Notice how the positive feelings are less intense and the negative feelings are more intense for prevention goals than for promotion goals. Given that complete achievement of a prevention goal is almost utopian, those intense negative feelings are constantly lurking in the background.

PRIORITIZING THE WRONG GOALS

Life goals, however, are complex and may contain both promotion and prevention features. Let's assume, for example, that my goal is to get an MBA. This goal has both promotion and prevention features. I made the decision to get an MBA because I want formal training in business management so I can learn new concepts, understand the research better, apply what I learn in a real setting, and help organizations and employees achieve their productivity goals. These are promotion features. On the other hand, I may choose to get an MBA because I don't want to lose my job, be passed over for a promotion, or not get a bonus this year. Those are prevention features.

Similarly, I may choose to work out to enjoy the benefits of cardiovascular fitness, muscle strength and flexibility, and the endorphin surge that leads to the runner's high (promotion features) or so that I don't look fat, I don't have to stop eating junk food, or I won't have a stroke when I am sixty (prevention features).

Our brains process positive information (recognizing the presence of something) faster and better than they process negative information (recognizing the absence of something). Therefore, when our brains focus on and prioritize the promotion features of a goal, they are more efficient processors. Our actions, thoughts, and feelings are consistent with positive perfectionism (striving toward the acquisition of something). Not only are we better at solving problems and overcoming obstacles, but we take more pleasure in our goal pursuit and enjoy better psychological health.

When our brains focus on and prioritize the prevention features of a goal, perfectionism turns negative (seeking the absence of something). Our actions become compulsions; our thoughts, obsessions; and our emotions, pangs of guilt. Our brain creates infinite loops of action, thoughts, and feelings to search for what is not there, which lead to the relentless criticism of self and others, obsession with order and detail, and preoccupation with rejection, characteristic of negative perfectionists.

Another way to understand the difference is to imagine that you are in a room and someone asked you to find a spider. You will look around, maybe for a very long time, but as soon as you find the spider your mission is accomplished. Now imagine that you go back to the room, and someone tells you to make sure there are no spiders in the room. You start looking around for spiders to make sure there aren't any. You scan the whole room and you don't see any, but you have to continue searching because a spider may have sneaked in through a crack when you were looking in the opposite direction. Even if you do find a spider, your work is not done. You need to keep looking endlessly because your goal is to ensure that there are no spiders in the room.

Brainblock Side Effects

In small doses, the effects of perfectionism may go unnoticed. But a large enough daily dose can have disastrous effects on your productivity, on your happiness, and even on your sex life! Perfectionism is a maze without an exit. It keeps you busy to no avail. You can keep going around and around trying to achieve the best you can, but it never seems enough.

What happens to perfectionists?

IDEAS GET TRAPPED INSIDE

Perfectionism is one of the main reasons ideas remain ghosts in your head instead of coming to life as convincing statements, forward-moving actions, or tangible products. Thinking about things thoroughly is not bad. Overthinking them is. Ideas need time to take form and to develop, just as embryos do. While an idea is still incubating in your head, perfectionism will never let it flourish. Perfectionism makes your ideas always seem untimely, unpolished, and unpopular. It keeps you *thinking* while others are *doing*.

A lot of people associate perfectionism with procrastination. While delaying the beginning of a task is characteristic of procrastination, delaying the end of one is a hallmark of perfectionism. Your product is never shiny enough. Your blog is never persuasive enough. Your cake is never fluffy enough. You may have all the great ideas in the world, and you may have tangible products ready to launch, but you keep tweaking them, adjusting them, and then tweaking them again, until they are past their prime. Perfectionism, unlike procrastination, is not about not starting something. It is about not finishing it because you are not ready to show it and share it. It isn't good enough yet . . . they may criticize it . . . they may dislike it . . . they may judge it . . . and worse, they may judge you.

THERE IS NO ONE ELSE WHO CAN DO IT

Perfectionists have difficulty delegating tasks to others because they worry they will have to redo everything anyway. They don't trust others. They become very worried when they assign someone else to do something, even if their intention was to free up some time for themselves. At the end, they will still have to look over the work someone else did for them again and again to make sure that it meets their standards.

Perfectionists forget that people have different styles and that making mistakes is inevitable. Anything you assign someone else to do will not be done the same way you would do it. And the bigger your magnifying glass is, the more cracks you will find. But the perfectionists get stuck on this very simple concept. They get very frustrated with the person they delegated the task to and they spend a lot of time trying to fix the supposedly fatal errors.

BEAT THE SPIRIT OUT OF OTHERS

Perfectionists set the bar for others too high and then expect them to jump over it. When they don't, they get disappointed. But they don't keep their disappointment to themselves. They begin to punish those who are not able to meet the highest standards. They push people beyond their limits and level of readiness, without explaining how and why something should be done. They stop being supportive and they don't focus on growth. They use criticism and derision, instead of constructive feedback and empathy.

Ask the children of perfectionistic parents to describe what it is like growing up constantly feeling that they are falling short of their families' standards. If you were looking for a source of self-doubt, here is one: perfectionistic parents with unreasonable expectations about what their children should be able to accomplish and a very vocal way of expressing their disappointment.

BEAT YOUR OWN SPIRIT

The odds that a perfectionist is happy with the outcome of an action are the same as the odds that the outcome is perfect. Perfectionists are trapped in an infinite loop of disappointment because, despite their efforts, their work never meets their standards. Imagine being constantly disappointed and dissatisfied with your inability to fulfill your own expectations.

To prevent this cycle of disappointment, perfectionists spend a lot of energy making sure that all the imperfections are fixed. That makes their anxiety go through the roof. The worry gets worse when the perfectionists present their work to others, praying that no one will find any flaws or mistakes and embarrass them.

Perfectionists respond to feedback with guilt and shame. They miss out on the benefits of constructive feedback. They focus on and obsess about the things that went wrong. They feel pride only when their results are perfect, which is never.

AND SOMETIMES BEAT IT TO A PULP

As if disappointment, anxiety, guilt, and shame weren't bad enough, perfectionism has been linked to a lot of other serious outcomes. Research shows that perfectionists tend to have more depression (*life is not perfect*), eating disorders like bulimia and anorexia nervosa (*my body is not perfect*), sexual dysfunction (*I am not the perfect lover*), lower self-esteem (*I am far from perfect*), and obsessive–compulsive disorder (*I will make things perfect or else . . .*). They are afraid of failing, losing control, and making mistakes. They have difficulty relating to other people. Either they feel constantly judged, which makes it hard for them to be in social situations, or they expect too much of others, which doesn't make them fun to be around. Perfectionists are more cynical, they have more stress, and they are less satisfied with themselves and with their lives in general.

Smashing the Brainblock

Far from perfect, the following well-established strategies will protect you from fussing over unnecessary concerns and help you refocus on what's important.

STRATEGY 1: ESTABLISH THE PRIORITIES

Perfectionism is a failure in prioritizing. What is secondary becomes primary. What is background becomes foreground. Wearing the right outfit takes precedence over enjoying the party. Setting up the silverware gets more attention than preparing the meal.

Prioritizing the prevention features of a goal over its promotion features results in a range of problems for perfectionists. When their brain is attuned to threats and losses instead of incentives and gains, actions focus on avoiding instead of achieving. Avoidance actions have a lower rate of success for accomplishing a goal.

The smart way to avoid the brainblock of negative perfectionism is to steer it instead toward its counterpart: productive action. Shift the nature of a task from prevention to promotion.

Look at the following table. The column on the left lists the kinds of actions you focus on when you have a promotion orientation. The column on the right lists actions you focus on when you maintain a prevention orientation. Use this table to first learn to recognize and identify what the priorities of your actions are, and then use Strategy 2 to train yourself to shift your actions from prevention to promotion.

PROMOTION ACTION	PREVENTION ACTION
Achieving order *I like things organized*	Avoiding disorder *I hate chaos*
Seeking feedback *I need a second opinion*	Avoiding criticism *I don't care what they have to say*
Producing/creating/ generating *I baked a cake*	Not making mistakes *It was the worst cake ever*
Including the essentials *I wrote my speech*	Including bells and whistles *I can't choose the right words*
Making the main point *I didn't make the deadline . . .*	Not leaving out details *. . . and here are all the reasons why*
Gaining knowledge *I don't know, but I will find out for you*	Appearing unknowledgeable *I don't think anybody knows that*
Informing others *This is what you should know*	Impressing others *Let me tell you what else I know*
Gaining mastery *My children challenge me to become a better parent*	Losing control *My children need to stop making unreasonable demands*
Assessing how much has been achieved *I have reached out to four clients today*	Assessing how much is missing *I haven't reached my quota of calls yet*

PROMOTION ACTION	PREVENTION ACTION
Experiencing joy *I am getting together with old friends I haven't seen in a while*	Avoiding shame/embarrassment *I hope they don't ask why I haven't moved forward with my business idea yet*
Getting a gold star *I want to get good reviews*	Not getting a red card *I don't want to get bad reviews*

STRATEGY 2: PROMOTE YOUR GOALS

You would be surprised how many of your goals or aspects of them are focused on prevention rather than promotion. For example, some of the reasons you are staying at your current job is because it provides you with financial security, with health insurance, with status, and with structure. You may hate your job, and it may be making your daily life a living hell, but if you lose it, there will be a handful of negative outcomes, starting with losing all those benefits just listed.

Prevention goals are hard to achieve. They place you on a treadmill without a stop button. Their achievement gives you little pleasure, and their pursuit is filled with fear, anxiety, guilt, and shame. Prevention goals are constant reminders of the negative aspects of our lives we wish to change or the negative prospects we hope to avoid, and as a result they can have a sweeping effect on our lives. The good news is that prevention goals can easily be changed into promotion goals.

STEP 1. Create a table with three columns. Label the first column "Prevention," the second column "Positive Outcomes," and the third column "Promotion."*

STEP 2. Identify your prevention goals. To find your prevention goals, think about all the things in your life that you don't like, you are forced to deal with, you are frustrated with, you would like to change, or you want to avoid. Prevention goals usually include negative terms, especially the word *not*. Write them down in column one.

STEP 3. Describe the positive outcome you would like to achieve. For each of the goals that you listed, think of all the good things that would happen if that problem were taken care of. Write those down in column two.

STEP 4. Rewrite the prevention goal as a promotion goal. Using the information in the first two columns, rewrite the goal as a promotion goal. Pick one of the positive outcomes you listed and create a new goal to address the same issue. Make sure the phrasing of your new goal does *not* include the word *not*!

STRATEGY 3: MICROMANAGE YOUR GOALS

Regardless of the size of the goal, the actions that will achieve it are small. Actions are tiny little bites, designed to consume the entire meal, the goal. Because of the rapid and imperceptible shifts in priorities that the

---

* Or you can download the one I made for you at SmashingTheBrainblocks .com.

brainblock of perfectionism may cause, micromanaging your actions will keep you on track to ensure you are working on the right goal. When you are immersed in a project, chained by a sequence of actions intended to bring that project to an end, check whether each action serves the purpose of the larger goal.

STEP 1. Before starting work on a project, ask yourself, What is my goal right now? State a simple and straight-forward goal. For example, my goal is to make dinner or my goal is to put together a presentation for work.

STEP 2. Begin the work. All your actions should align with your goals. Making your intention and your actions consistent will also prevent multitasking.

STEP 3. When you find yourself obsessing or fretting over details, stop and restate your goal. Make sure your actions are not serving a different goal. Remind yourself of what you are trying to accomplish. If your goal was to make dinner, the outcome should be food at the table, not a three-star Michelin meal. If your goal was to put together a presentation, the outcome should be a presentation with enough useful content tightly organized in a way that makes sense. It is not to deliver an Emmy-worthy performance. A generous applause may still give you a sense of accomplishment!

STEP 4. Every forty-five minutes take a break and restate your goal. This will help you avoid veering off the main point and into the land of details or into the realm of a different goal.

STRATEGY 4: COUNT BLESSINGS, NOT BLEMISHES

When you start developing a panic attack about how far from perfect your work or your life or your relationship or your outfit is, stop and appreciate what you already have.

Perfectionism is often motivated by the fear of not being good enough, not having done enough, not being appreciated enough. But if you have gotten as far as to be concerned about shortcomings and imperfections in your work, then you must have done something right. In fact, you must have done a few things quite well.

The same rule applies to your evaluation of other people. When you start worrying that others are falling short of your expectations, look back and appreciate what they *are* doing well. There must be a reason they entered your world to begin with.

One of my favorite TED talks is "Every Kid Needs a Champion," delivered by Rita Pierson.[6] Pierson is an educator who has been teaching students who are considered challenged learners. One day she gave her class a twenty-question quiz. One student missed eighteen. Pierson wrote +2 on the quiz, put a smiley face next to it, and gave it back. The student asked her if that was an F. She said it was. He asked, "Why did you put a smiley face?" She said, "Because you're on a roll! You got two right. You didn't miss them all!" What a great example of counting blessings! Think about the difference that a +2 can make compared to a –18 for that child.

So, instead of fussing over the missing parts, take inventory of what you have already accomplished. Instead of criticizing others for their shortcomings, praise them for their contributions. And instead of worrying about what others will think about your failure to achieve perfection, fantasize about the praise they will give you for your efforts.

STRATEGY 5: START WITH MILESTONES, NOT WITH END POINTS

Perfect implies ultimate, final, best, unsurpassable, unbeatable. What are the implications of seeking perfection for progress and innovation?

Imagine if the creative team of Apple said back in October 2001, "We will create this awesome digital music player that can put '1,000 songs in your pocket' and that's our end goal."[7] The iCraze would have stopped at the first-generation iPod. Not only are we now several generations down the line, but we also have available dozens of other variations on the same theme. All the subsequent Apple products came to life because the first iPod was not considered an end point, but a milestone. The team didn't stop at the iPod, but they also didn't feel disappointed that their first gadget would be very modest compared to the iPhone 6. It was just a step in a series of many, and something to still be proud of.

Champions and pioneers do not set end points. They set milestones. Their goal is to keep up and do a little better every time. Given that perfection is elusive and the closer you get to it, the farther away it seems to be, get in the habit of setting milestones instead of end points. Milestones are attainable and specific. Milestones take into account where you are now and how far you can go in the near future. If you would like to complete a marathon but are currently unable to run a 5K, then the shorter race is your starting point. A 10K race and then a 21K half marathon may be your next milestones as you work your way up to the full 42K marathon. If you are writing a book and you have never been published before, consider publishing an article first, before running yourself into the ground trying to write the bestselling novel of the year.

Milestones create promotion goals. They help you create concrete, well-defined goals, as opposed to using abstract, undefined standards. They also help you monitor your overall progress, so you can avoid the brainblocks of procrastination or impatience. Milestones are concrete, whereas end points are moving targets.

What are your milestones?

STEP 1. Identify an important life goal.

STEP 2. Set five specific milestones for your goal. Make them concrete, specific, and attainable.

STEP 3. Focus on your first milestone. After you reach your first milestone, go back to your list, review it, and make changes based on your experience achieving the first milestone.

STEP 4. Repeat Step 3 for each milestone.

STEP 5. When you reach your final milestone, assess how close you are to the end point. If you have reached it, congratulate yourself and focus on a new goal. If not, then create another set of milestones, and stay put. Remind yourself to count blessings!

STRATEGY 6: SET LIMITS IN STONE

Setting limits is a technique guaranteed to make you snap out of obsessive, perfectionistic mode. Decide how much of your resources you are willing to expend for any given project you are working on.

A few years ago, my colleagues and I were applying for a $4.5 million grant from the Centers for Disease Control and Prevention (CDC). The stakes were high, so we were compelled to create a perfect proposal. I remember that for weeks we were going through numerous revisions and endless iterations. It had gotten to the point at which we were making changes in one version that we would change back to the original wording in the next. Lucky for us, the limits were imposed to us by external powers: a rigid deadline and specific page limit. Otherwise, my guess is we would still be working on it.

In real life, the limits are more flexible and more obscure. And unless you set them on your own, you can always take a little more time, make a little more effort, and spend a little more money, to make your work a little better and move it a little further. Protect your resources by putting an end to the obsessiveness! Here is how to better manage your five most valuable resources (TIMES):

a. **Time.** Set a time limit. Create a deadline. And make it a drop deadline. No matter how much a product, a project, a speech, or a pickup line can be perfected, it is more important that you actually deliver it.

b. **Information.** Set a limit to the amount of information you need, to how much research you need to do before you feel that you have covered enough ground, and to how much knowledge you have gained on a topic.

c. **Money.** Set a limit to the amount of money you are willing to spend to make something perfect. Whether it is your appearance, your home decor, your personal development, your kids' material comfort, you have to set your own credit limit.

d. **Energy.** Set a limit to how much effort you are willing to put forth before you run yourself to the ground, before you start feeling exhausted, fatigued, and demoralized. This includes mental and emotional energy as well.

e. **Support.** Set a limit to how much help you need from others and how much you can give back. You can get advice, feedback, input, and perspectives ad nauseam and never really get anything done. At the same time, do not get caught up in other people's perfectionism by supplying them with unlimited support.

STRATEGY 7: GAIN PERSPECTIVE

One of the most effective ways to untangle yourself from the web of perfectionism is to gain perspective. Looking to create the perfect conditions, to produce the best outcome, to provide the ideal services, and to generate a flawless product keeps you locked in an infinite loop. You begin to process the same facts, the same data, the same images, the same letters on a screen, and the same ideas in your head and, as a result, you begin to obsess.

What you need at these moments is perspective. Immersed in your work, you may not realize that your priorities are shifting from promotion to prevention. "I didn't add information about this sector of the market in my report" or "I didn't include my two months' work experience at the local newspaper on my CV." There will be no end to how much more you could do to achieve the perfect outcome.

Here are some ways to gain perspective:

a. **Take a break.** Stop working on the task at hand. Give yourself time to cool down from the overheating and exhaustion that perfectionism causes. Give your brain some rest, and let it do some unconscious processing.

b. **Shift your focus.** Walk away from your project and do something different. If you are working on something conceptual, like the outline of a book, do something physical, like washing the dishes or walking the dog. If you are working on something physical, like putting together an IKEA dresser, step away briefly and do something social, like calling a friend. Then go back to your project.

c. **Gain another perspective.** Show someone else your work in progress. Ask her to review your work, to look at your project, or to help you brainstorm. Not only are you taking a break and shifting your focus, but you are enriching your work by looking at it from a new angle.

Gaining a fresh perspective enables you to focus on the whole instead of getting lost in the details. It will give you a different appreciation for what you have already done, and align your actions with a promotion orientation.

NEGATIVITY

The Fine Art of Complaining

Of all the brainblocks, negativity is queen. It is a mega-block. It stops you from taking action at all three stages of your success path. It can interfere with setting, pursuing, and achieving your goals.

During goal setting, negativity holds you back from daring to dream, to desire, to aspire. It turns your dreams into nightmares. Like a cannonball it can shatter your optimism into shards of broken hope.

During goal pursuit, it blocks you from working diligently and consistently toward your goal. It paralyzes you insidiously like a potent neurotoxin. And through your words and actions, it can also spread to others around you, like a highly infectious disease.

And when you achieve a goal, negativity will shift your focus from celebrating your success to doing damage control, worrying about the longevity and genuineness of your success, and thinking about all the additional work and responsibility that comes with success.

How do negative people achieve their goals? What kinds of actions do they take? Negativity is the fine art of complaining. Instead of focusing their energy on learning, creating, and putting to practice, negative people focus on complaining about themselves, about others, and about the future.

Any time you see absence, lack, scarcity, deficiency, or unavailability around you, you will get exactly that: nothing. The perception of lack and absence that is characteristic of negativity extends to many aspects of life: lack of money, options, love, trust, friends, and so on. Everywhere you look, you see nothing. Seeing nothing will prompt you to do nothing. Your motivation drops to zero, and your energy is completely depleted.

Welcome to the world of negativity.

The Confessional

Jackie was spending her days taking care of her (not that) elderly father. He didn't really need 24/7 care, but she was convinced that if she left him alone for too long, something very bad would happen. Her father hadn't been working for a while. He was on disability because of an injury he sustained that left him unable to work but able to take care of himself.

Before Jackie moved in with her father, she was studying to be a nurse. She was one of the most reliable, responsible, and perceptive students in her class. But because of the circumstances, she dropped out of school and became full-time nurse to her father.

That was five years ago. Jackie is stuck at home now. She can't afford to go back to school. She still owes a lot of money in student loans for all her years of school. Besides, applying to nursing schools would be a moot point. She would be rejected at the first cut, given her history of dropping out. Not to mention that even in the very unlikely event that she were accepted, it would be impossible for her to get back into the groove of academic life and be a good student.

She knows that finding a job is not an option either. Who would hire her with no work experience, no specialized skills, and a big five-year gap on her life's CV? She did go to two interviews about four years ago, and neither of them amounted to anything, so why expect that things would be better now? Actually, even a life coach she randomly met once told her that her odds of getting a job were low.

Her health is also getting worse. She hasn't been working out, she hasn't been eating well, and she hasn't been sleeping regularly. She feels tired and depressed all the time, and things can only go downhill from here.

And as for her love life, it is limited to TV dramas and romantic comedies. Who would date someone like her? Men don't notice her anymore, and on the rare occasion a man looks in her direction, it's because she looks so common that they must have mistaken her for someone else.

This is Jackie speaking. And she can go on and on about how much her life sucks. And that's where all her energy goes. That's negativity!

Spotting the Brainblock

The primary action of negativity is complaining. Complaining includes bemoaning, judging, and catastrophizing.

Primary Action:

I complain

And these are the three major symptoms of negativity:

1. YOU BEMOAN . . .

A lot
You swim in a pool of self-pity. You feel sorry for yourself. You feel more comfortable wallowing in self-pity than taking action to change.

About how little you get back
You feel rejected, wronged, unappreciated, unloved, untrusted. Regardless of how much you do for others, how much effort you put into relationships, how giving and forgiving you are, you feel you don't get due credit. Your kindness goes unnoticed and your efforts unrecognized.

And how unfair life is

Your life seems like a losing battle. You feel drowned in injustice, failure, weakness, attack, and punishment. You often feel victimized by life, by the circumstances, and by others.

And that affects your mood

You are chronically in a bad mood. You feel worried, alarmed, resentful, disappointed, and bitter.

And the mood of others

You develop an exceptional ability to ruin a good moment. When you are with others, you fish for sympathy. The main topic of the conversation is "poor me." You will talk about how no one cares about you, how harshly they are treating you at work, how sick you have been feeling, how much weight you have gained, how your life is going nowhere, how stuck you are.

2. YOU JUDGE . . .

Quickly

You like to pass judgment fast. You tend to spot people's flaws and shortcomings immediately. You think you know right away who lacks skill, who lacks decency, who lacks compassion, who lacks humility.

Selectively

You tend to notice and remember a person's shortcomings only. You focus on what other people are doing or saying wrong, how little they know, and what skills they lack. You ignore good qualities and honest effort.

All inclusively

You judge both people you know personally, like family and friends, and people you don't even know, like a celebrity's lifestyle or a politician's career decisions. You extend the same kind of overcritical attitude to everyone.

Openly

You are very willing to point out flaws and weaknesses. If your position permits, you will tell someone what he is doing wrong, even if he didn't ask you. But you're very stingy with compliments and praise.

As well as behind their backs

You also like to talk about others when they are not present and use the opportunity to criticize their choices, their attitude, their girlfriends, and their hair color with the same passion and dedication.

Unnecessarily

You criticize others often about minor, unimportant, and petty things.

But conclusively

You pick one shortcoming and judge the whole person by that.

And at a societal level

In its more intellectual and sublime form, your negativity comes across as opinion or cynicism. You have things to say about large social groups, organizations, governments, and even entire nations. You don't trust people and institutions. You see no good intentions, only ulterior motives.

In general, you are likely to be seen nagging, criticizing, blaming, and gossiping.

3. YOU PREDICT . . .

A grim future
You act as if you knew what will happen in the future, as if you could foresee the outcomes. And you foresee catastrophes. In your imaginary crystal ball you see failure and suffering.

You see gloom and doom everywhere
You focus only on the negative: The economy is tanking, unemployment is soaring, petty crime is on the rise, global warming is approaching faster than expected, the number of endangered species is growing, strains of flu have become more vaccine resistant, and people are dying everywhere.

So you live in fear
The fear of a grim future is paralyzing. You make mountains out of molehills. Small setbacks seem like insurmountable obstacles. Disaster lurks around the corner waiting to grab you.

And you want to protect yourself
You get discouraged from taking action because it could go wrong. Your fortune-telling ability tells you it's not the

right time to take risks or make changes. Don't ask your boss for a raise because she will say no anyway. Don't change jobs now because you will never find something good in this economy. Don't even think about a new career at your age because then you will never retire. Don't use the Internet to buy things because your identity will be stolen. Don't sign up for online dating because only trolls respond to those ads.

And to protect others

You make it your mission to warn others about unfavorable odds, hidden traps, and unexpected turns of events, so they too can abort their mission before it is too late.

And you end up putting a damper on their plans

Someone wants to start her own business? You will share a story about someone you know who failed. Someone else wants to go back to school? You will inform him that college graduates have the highest unemployment rates. She wants to leave her job? She should be happy to have one.

Behind the Brainblock: Failure in Reasoning

ORGANIZING OUR WORLD

What makes people live on the dark side of the moon; what makes them see the glass half empty? Is there something about the way their brain processes information that affects their outlook on things? Where is negativity generated in the brain?

Negativity is a failure in reasoning. Our brains are rapid learning machines. They receive, store, process, analyze, synthesize, and generate vast amounts of information. We eventually use that information to draw conclusions, make decisions, respond to situations, and take actions.

To make sense of all of the information, we need to keep it organized and accessible. Our brains start looking for patterns and similarities in the data, and we slowly start building theories. Theories are general and hypothetical statements about pretty much anything, including who we are, how the world works, and what the meaning of life is.

We use our theories to explain and predict what's happening around us or within us. For example, doctors use their theories to diagnose and treat their patients. Mechanics use their theories to fix your car. Teachers use their theories to improve their students' performance. Coaches use their theories to train their athletes better. Chefs use their theories to create gourmet dishes. And negative people use their theories to make their lives a living hell.

Theories influence the thoughts and ideas we have, the opinions and judgments we form, the attributions and predictions we make, and they guide our present and future actions. Good theories help us make better decisions in the present and more accurate predictions about the future. But what makes a theory good?

Good theories are based on facts. Facts include evidence from direct observations, past experience, or prior knowledge. Good theories are a product of good reasoning. They should follow the rules of logic. Good theories are also testable theories. You should be able to prove them or disprove them.

But we don't always develop good theories because we don't always follow these rules. We don't test our theories, we don't consider all the facts, we use emotion instead of logic, we become too attached, and we turn our theories to convictions. What makes our reasoning fail? What causes the glitch?

Because of the multiple and increasing demands to solve a wide range of problems in our daily lives, our brains have streamlined the process of decision making by developing algorithms capable of shuffling through the enormous amounts of data we constantly receive and store in our memory. These algorithms are called *heuristics*, and they are shortcuts or overlearned methods of selecting, organizing, and using information. Heuristics are cognitive response styles, or habits of thinking, if you will. But just like there are good and bad behavioral habits, there are good and bad thinking habits. And those bad thinking habits cause the glitches. Cognitive scientists call these bad thinking habits *cognitive biases*. These biases affect the theories we build, and they can lead to the wrong conclusions, the wrong decisions, and consequently the wrong actions.

THE COGNITIVE BIASES

What are some of the most important cognitive biases and how do they contribute to the development and maintenance of negativity?

BELIEF BIAS: I BELIEVE IT, THEREFORE IT'S TRUE

Belief bias happens when you accept as true and logical those statements that sound believable. When you become too attached to your theories, you don't bother to check the facts. Your strong belief makes your theory sound true, and it eliminates the need to search for evidence. Your conclusions are not based on whether something makes sense logically but instead on whether it conforms to your expectations. Instead of relying on facts to guide your thinking and your actions, you rely on your beliefs.

One of the most controversial subjects in medical literature is the spontaneous remission of cancer. Spontaneous remission is the unexpected and untreated shrinking of a cancerous tumor. You can imagine that with cancer having jumped to number two among the leading causes of death in the United States according to CDC statistics, the topic of spontaneous remission is one of great interest to all stakeholders: patients, families, and friends; the medical community; and everyone else.

A couple of years ago, there was an interesting discussion on the topic of spontaneous cancer remission on an online forum for cancer survivors. A woman had posted that about twenty years earlier her husband had been diagnosed with three glioblastoma multiforme tumors, a malignant and aggressive type of brain tumor. The treatment options included chemotherapy, radiation, and surgery, the last of which would give him the highest chance of survival, at 30 percent. For various reasons, he chose not to have any kind of treatment and instead maintained a positive outlook and a healthy lifestyle. Two years later, he went back to the doctor, at which time the tumors were gone—spontaneous remission of glioblastoma! Now, how do you explain that?

Was this a miracle? Was this an act of God? A religious person might say yes because this explanation is consistent with his beliefs. And the investigation stops there, followed perhaps by a few gratitude prayers, a promise for redemption, and several acts of kindness toward others. From his perspective, this is a perfectly plausible explanation: "I believe that God performs medical miracles, and, therefore, I will accept that this was an act of God." This is a one example of belief bias.

But the physician's response would be, "There are no such things as medical miracles. In fact, tumors don't just disappear. This person is lying." This is another type of belief bias.

Now, contrast these perspectives with a medical researcher's perspective. The medical researcher does not believe that the remission was due to divine intervention, nor does she believe that the person is lying. Instead, she starts looking for a different explanation. Were the spots on the scans misinterpreted as tumors? Were the tumors misdiagnosed as malignant? Did the doctor who made the original diagnosis accidentally mix up patient records? Have there been similar cases of spontaneous remission of glioblastoma reported in the medical literature? Was there something unique about this patient's immune system that prevented the tumors from growing? Was there something about his diet or lifestyle that facilitated the cancer remission? From the medical researcher's perspective, answering these questions is more important in understanding and explaining this very rare but lifesaving medical phenomenon. She demonstrates no belief bias.

How does belief bias build negativity? If your theory about yourself, other people, or the world is that you are bound to fail, people are mean or stupid, and the world is a dangerous place, these are the kinds of conclusions that you will be coming to when dealing with challenges in your own life.

CONFIRMATION BIAS:
FINDING WHAT YOU ARE LOOKING FOR

We want our theories to be right. Confirmation bias stems from the strong need to protect our theories from the sharp claws of evidence that can tear them apart. In contrast to belief bias, confirmation bias is more scientific. When you commit confirmation bias, you actually do take the facts into consideration . . . but selectively. You tend to register only those facts that support your theories and ignore anything else. As a result, your belief in your theory, regardless of whether it is right or wrong, becomes stronger and stronger because you continue to gather only the evidence that supports it.

Confirmation bias happens every day and everywhere. If I believe that women are bad drivers, every time I see a woman driving slow in the left lane, I will remind myself of how right I am. But if I see a man driving, I will pass him on the left and move on without further thought. If you think that your new employee is incompetent, you will start creating a problem log. Therefore, all you see about this person is a long list of problems, and you can justify firing her, even though you don't do that for any other employee.

Nowhere does confirmation bias cause more damage than in the courtroom. Researchers consistently find evidence of confirmation bias in the way juries, judges, and experts make decisions. When a suspect is identified, those in charge of examining the evidence tend to look for information that incriminates the suspect and overlook information that absolves him. The effect is so powerful that a little bit of instruction can turn into a lot of bias. In one study five experts were called to match a set of fingerprints found on the scene with those of a suspect. They were told that the suspect had been wrongly accused. Expecting that the fingerprints shouldn't match, four out of the five experts declared that they didn't match. What the experts weren't told was that several years earlier, they all had been asked to look at the same prints, and at that time all five had decided they were a match![1] Did they become better investigators over the years or did a little piece of additional information influence their judgment? Confirmation bias can ruin innocent lives.

Imagine that your theory is that you have bad luck in life. Each time something bad happens, you will register that fact as confirmation that indeed you have bad luck. Did someone scratch your car in the parking lot? Bad luck. Did you lose a $20 bill? Bad luck. Did you break your glasses? Bad luck. What about all the times when you parked without getting your car scratched, or when all your money stayed in your wallet, or your glasses remained intact? Aren't they evidence of good luck? But you don't have a good luck theory. You have a bad luck theory, and those instances don't fit in it. Therefore, you ignore them.

BASE-RATE NEGLECT: IGNORING THE ODDS
Things happen. Good things happen and bad things happen. But we don't always know how often they happen, so we assume. The term that scientists use to describe how often something occurs in a population is *base rate*. For example, the base rate of depression in the general population is about 10 percent. So, if you ever said, "Everyone gets depressed," you would have been wrong.

We tend to ignore base rates and make assumptions about the frequency of things based on our own experiences (see the next bias). We build our theories based on the wrong proportions, and we, therefore, end up overestimating or underestimating how often something occurs.

In March 2014 a report came out indicating that the

number of millionaires in the United States had hit a record high.[2] In fact, the report stated that 9.63 million households in the United States reported net worth of $1 million or more. That sounds like an enormous amount of households. Is your household one of them? Why not? Why aren't you a millionaire yet? Have you been slacking? Everyone else seems to be doing quite well.

Let's look at the facts again. How many households are there in the United States? According to the 2010 census, there are 116.7 million households. The 9.63 million households of millionaires represent about 8 percent of all households. This means that less than 10 percent of all households reported a net worth of over a million. Another way to look at this statistic is that 92 percent of households reported a net worth of *less* than a million. By chance alone, you are one of the people who make less than a million. Now, if you were curious why you are not worth more than $5 million, that percentage of households is only 1 percent. And those who are worth over $25 million make up 0.1 percent, leaving 99.9 percent of the population netting under $25 million. So you are safe! Not a slacker![*]

If all you hear in the news is how the number of millionaires has skyrocketed and you are unaware of the base rate, then you may start feeling like the loser who has been left behind. The wrong base rate can lead you to the wrong conclusion.

---

[*] This is not to discourage you from becoming a millionaire. This is to comfort you from your own self-criticism, if you are not there yet.

AVAILABILITY BIAS: THE CONVENIENCE FACTOR

Availability bias means that you make decisions based on how easy it is to think of relevant examples of something. You begin to explain things based on what you know really well, what you heard or read recently, and how well you remember something. You estimate how likely something is to happen based on how easy it is to think of related examples. If you recently heard that there was a flu outbreak in your state, the next time you feel warm you will start suspecting that you caught the flu.

One of the most common disorders that medical and psychology students experience is *intern's syndrome*. Intern's syndrome is an epidemic, especially among second- and third-year students. The symptoms vary from mild to severe, from acute to chronic, and from physical to psychiatric. In some cases, emergency interventions are necessary. What causes this peculiar disorder?

As students start learning more about the names, symptoms, etiologies, and treatments of diseases and disorders, they begin to actually experience the symptoms of these illnesses and may go as far as to seek treatment. What really happens is that students develop a new theoretical framework to understand the human body, which they use to explain what may be normal physical and emotional reactions. When a student has just learned that lack of energy and poor sleep are symptoms of depression, she is going to give herself a diagnosis of depression as soon as she notices these symptoms. Surely, her lack of energy and poor sleep may suggest that she is depressed. But do you think there may be other reasons why a medical student may be losing sleep and feeling tired?

Availability bias doesn't affect only medical students. It affects all health and mental health professionals and can lead to serious errors in judgment and decision making. Providers may inadvertently make diagnoses and choose treatments based on more easily accessible information, like things they know well but may be outdated, or on things they read recently in a medical journal, but may be too limited in scope at this point.

How does this glitch create negativity? Negative people have negative theories. They are drawn to negative information (confirmation bias), which they can access a lot more easily when they make decisions, because that's all they have available. If you are brewing negativity, you will drink negativity.

ANCHORING: JUDGING BOOKS BY THEIR COVERS

Anchoring is the tendency to rely on first impressions when making decisions. Your first experience with an event, a situation, or a person sets the tone forever. You set your future expectations based on that first impression, without deviating much. If you set the bar low from the beginning, you won't raise it much later. If you set it high, you won't move it down later. Anchoring gets you stuck in a limited range of options. Initial experiences create permanent perceptions. Preliminary evidence determines final decisions. Anchoring can affect your life so broadly. It can influence what kind of work you do, how much money you make, how high your mortgage is, who you marry, how many children you have, how many vacations you take, and even how long you expect to live.

A great example of anchoring is the popular TV game show *The Price Is Right*. In this show, contestants have to guess the prices of merchandise to win a prize. In one segment of the show, four lucky contestants are selected from the audience and are asked to estimate the price of an item. Each player calls out a price. The winner is the person whose guess is closest to the actual price of the item, without overbidding. Let's say that the prize is a laptop computer. Player 1 guesses it costs $1,200. Player 2 says $1,100. Player 3 says it's probably more expensive, like $1,249. And Player 4 says $1,250, just a dollar more than Player 3, to guarantee a win, if the laptop is indeed above $1,250. Did you notice something? The price that Player 1 called out anchored everyone else's answer. The other three contestants used that initial guess to determine their own bids. Their bids didn't vary much from the first player's estimate. Alas, if the laptop were an HP Slatebook 14, priced at $379.99, they would all lose and blame Player 1 for anchoring them too high!*

---

* If you would like to know more about how to win on *The Price Is Right*, along with other cool facts that make for great party conversation, check out Ben Blatt's strategy on Slate.com.

HINDSIGHT BIAS: I KNEW IT ALL ALONG!

Hindsight bias refers to our perceptions of events and situations for which we already know the outcome. These are the judgments and opinions we form about things that have already happened. It reflects our tendency to exaggerate the probability that we could have predicted the outcome correctly if we had made our prediction before the event occurred. In other words, hindsight bias is our ability to predict past events with great precision. This is a very common bias, and popular wisdom has captured it in the phrase "hindsight is always twenty/twenty."

A couple of years ago, a twenty-three-year-old woman brought malpractice charges against a licensed chemical dependency and mental health counselor. The woman claimed that she sought treatment for an eating disorder. She was admitted as an inpatient to the facility owned by the counselor and his wife. When she could no longer cover the cost, she was transferred to the counselor's unlicensed transitional housing facility, where she served as a house monitor. Her condition worsened, and eventually she was fired and discharged from the facility. The charges included allegations that her treatment was interrupted prematurely, causing worsening of her symptoms and significant emotional distress. What do you think was the court's ruling?

This is usually how researchers study hindsight bias. They give half of the study participants a hypothetical scenario and the other half a hypothetical scenario plus the outcome. They ask the first group to predict the outcome. They ask the second group what they would have predicted the outcome to be, if they hadn't been given it ahead of time. Consistently, participants in the second group, who are told the outcome beforehand, say that they would have predicted the outcome correctly. Participants who don't know the outcome at all vary more widely in their predictions. Are those people who don't know the results ahead of time less smart or less clairvoyant? They are just less biased.

So if I don't reveal to you the court's ruling in the malpractice just cited, half of you may say the ruling was in favor of the plaintiff and half in favor of the defendant. If I tell you what the ruling was, most of you will say that this was the same exact ruling you would have guessed too.

The most disconcerting finding about hindsight bias is that not only are we overconfident in our predictions of the past but our memories get twisted as well. In one type of hindsight bias study, researchers ask participants to answer a factual question (for example, How old was Nelson Mandela when he died?). The researchers record the participants' answers. Later, they give half of the participants the right answer (Nelson Mandela died at age ninety-five), but not the other half. Then they ask everyone to recall from memory how they answered the question. Participants who weren't told the correct answer are better at remembering their original responses more accurately. A participant who thought that Mandela died at age seventy-nine will say seventy-nine again. Those who are given the correct answer are worse at remembering their original answers. In fact, they make up answers that resemble the correct answer more than their own original answers. So a participant who thought that Mandela died at seventy-nine thinks that his original answer was eighty-nine, after he finds out that Mandela died at ninety-five.

Hindsight bias distorts our memories of the past, but it can also destroy our expectations of the future. Negativity is characterized by the tendency to make catastrophic predictions of the future, which has its origin in hindsight bias. If you are able to predict so well (after the fact) all the bad things that happen, you are definitely able to foresee doom and gloom in the future as well.

VISCERAL BIAS: I FEEL, THEREFORE I AM . . . RIGHT

Finally, another bias that can influence our decision making is the power of our own emotions. Feelings override evidence. How we feel in the moment determines how we judge a person or a situation. We judge things that make us feel good as more important, necessary, or valuable. We judge things that make us feel bad as threatening, hostile, or worthless.

Marketers understand well the influence of emotions on consumer behavior.[3] They know, for example, that:

- The more emotionally appealing an ad, the higher the brand sales.

- Consumers tend to buy products based on the emotional appeal of an ad rather than the ad's content.
- The more positive the emotions toward a brand, the stronger the customer trust and loyalty.
- According to neuroimaging studies, the parts of the brain that involve emotion are more active when choosing products than the parts that process information.

That's why companies strive to make emotional connections between their products and their consumers. And they do that by wrapping products in beautiful packages, photographing their products next to gorgeous models or breathtaking landscapes, describing them in words that go straight to your heart, and telling inspiring and heartfelt stories about those who use their products.

Visceral bias can distort your objectivity in either direction. If your emotions are generally positive, you will overestimate your abilities, underestimate risks, minimize the impact of errors, and exaggerate gains. If your emotions are generally negative, you flip your judgments: You underestimate your ability, you overestimate risk, you exaggerate consequences, and you minimize gains.

Brainblock Side Effects

Negativity drains your spirit, cripples your motivation, and damages your efforts. Not only does it undermine your potential but it can single-handedly destroy your physical and mental health, your relationships, your career, and, most important, your quality of life.

Negative people lose their ability to dream. And while negativity can cause serious damage to your dreams, it works like fertilizer for your nightmares. It blows your fears out of proportion. It is the bestselling author of worst-case scenarios.

DISTRUST: NO ONE I CAN RELY ON

Imagine living in a world where you can't have faith in anyone. People seem careless, inconsiderate, hostile, insincere, and antisocial. You become suspicious of everyone and everything. You can't trust people to keep their ends of bargains. You expect that they will fail you, betray you, abandon you, or mock you. You are not able to form deep connections with people because you never feel secure.

At a different level, you miss out on opportunities to learn from and collaborate with other people. You reject what they have to say because you think they are not good at what they do, or they don't agree with you, or they don't have your best interest at heart. They are probably trying to manipulate you, poke fun at you, or sell you something. The distrust extends to everyone. The doctor's medical advice is dubious because she is not board certified. The plumber overestimated the cost for repairs to swindle some money out of you. The teacher doesn't really care about your child's learning difficulties. The neighbors refuse to keep up their house, which makes yours lose value. Your husband doesn't follow through with his promises, your children need constant supervision to stay on the right path, and you can't really count on your friends to be there when you need them. No one is safe from the web of distrust.

LEARNED HELPLESSNESS: NOTHING I CAN DO

Negativity leads to passivity. If you don't believe you can change something, you won't try. Negative people are much more likely to anticipate failure. They experience learned helplessness—the belief that you don't have the power to change your situation. There is no action that will get you out of the rut, that will bring an end to your suffering, or that will prevent failure. As a result, there is no reason to make any effort, because your efforts will hit a brick wall and you will continue suffering.

Many people live in this state of learned helplessness. They stay in jobs they hate, they stay in relationships with people they don't love, or they live in places they detest. When the question of change comes up, the answer is a resounding *there is nothing I can do*. Do you see the self-fulfilling prophecy? When you think you can't accomplish something, you won't try. And if you don't try, you won't accomplish it.

PESSIMISM: LACK OF HOPE = LACK OF ACTION

Killing hope also kills dreams. More and more research studies are starting to show the benefits of optimism on physical health and emotional well-being. Optimistic people have fewer emotional problems, like depression and anxiety. They also seem to recover faster from illnesses and they view themselves as being healthier than pessimistic people.

Negativity is characterized by profound pessimism. The glass always looks half empty. Where there is opportunity for growth, you see risk for failure. Where there is praise, you see poor judgment. Where there is an invitation to display your creativity, you see the threat of exposing your lack of originality. Not expecting anything positive to happen in the future can be devastating. But most important, it prevents you from taking action because you expect that nothing will change as a result of your actions. You can see the obstacles, the traps, and the threats ahead of you, but you can't see past them. That's where you stop. Why continue when there is nothing behind the wall?

ISOLATION: NO ONE
LIKES A SOURPUSS

Negative people like to warn others about how unfair and dangerous life can be. They share stories of failure, incompetence, betrayal, and wretchedness. But that doesn't make you the life of the party. You may indeed know many people who failed in their careers, who lost money, whose fate turned, whose marriage fell apart. But bemoaning, forewarning, and catastrophizing doesn't make you good company. It makes you a bore and a downer. It pushes people away. People cannot put up with it for long. Eventually, they will keep you at bay to protect themselves from your toxic presence.

COLLUSION: FOLLY FOR TWO

There will be others, however, who will gladly listen to your lamentations and share your distorted worldview. You will commiserate with each other about how difficult and unjust life is, and how uncaring and malicious other people can be. You will together talk about how stuck and frustrated you feel, but you won't do much to change the situation. Instead of encouraging each other to take action, you will be adding fuel to each other's fire. You will stay in the pit of the negativity vortex together. Although they say that misery loves company, the truth is that misery loves miserable company. As comforting as it feels, these are not the kind of people you want to be around. You have nothing to learn from them. They don't inspire you, they don't challenge you, and they don't help you grow. Instead, they charge your negativity. They become another set of roadblocks.

CRIMINAL BEHAVIOR: KILLING OTHER PEOPLE'S DREAMS

Negativity stumps growth. Few plants grow in the dark and even fewer in arid land. This is the kind of environment you are creating for those around you. And while it's OK for you to kill your own dreams, it is not fair to infringe on other people's hopes and aspirations. When you present the world as hostile, people as undependable, and dreams as fantasies, you are infusing those around you with fear, resentment, and pessimism.

Think about the implications that these unhelpful ideas can have on the people close to you. Think about how the tone you set can influence who your children will become and what they will decide to do in the future. When you present them a world devoid of opportunities, they will not seek any. When you spend your energy judging, whining, and resenting—instead of supporting, encouraging, and inspiring—you are setting limits for the people in your life, and they will remain small. Years later, they will be equally resentful, pessimistic, and critical because their dreams were killed before they even hatched. Then it's their turn to pass that onto their own children.

DEPRESSION:
NO LIGHT AT THE END, JUST A DARK TUNNEL

A chronically negative person lives on the brink of depression. Negative people have all the prerequisites to become depressed. The resentment, the isolation, the pessimism, and the loss of social connection all contribute to create a joyless and painful existence. Add a little bit of self-doubt and a touch of rigidity to negativity and you have the best recipe for clinical depression.

Depression is characterized by the inability to feel and express joy. Depression stops people from taking action. They lose their momentum and vitality and become uncharged. They start falling behind on important life tasks, they lose track of their goals and dreams, they see no meaning behind their efforts, and they become nihilistic. Eventually, they are faced with the fact that they have not accomplished what they wanted, which confirms their theory that life is tough and success a utopia. This fuels their depression and negativity even more, and a vicious circle is created.

Smashing the Brainblock

If you want to achieve success, you have to defeat negativity. Negativity keeps you small and stalled. It's a one-way tunnel to a dark, depressive place. But it doesn't have to be so. Negativity is reversible. It requires challenging your reasoning, looking at the facts, gathering data, and doing what is necessary to keep a positive outlook.

STRATEGY 1: PRACTICE GRATITUDE

One of the most effective ways to defeat negativity is to shift your focus from the bad to the good.

Do you ever watch the news? I have stopped. In fact, I started calling it the *Bad News*. If you made a list of all the stories that the newscasters present and then categorized them as positive, negative, or neutral, what do you think the ratio of good to bad to neutral would be? A bank was robbed, a woman was raped, a child was bullied, a public official was accused of racketeering, a foreign nation is dabbling in nuclear weapons. . . . When do you ever hear that four hundred thousand banks robbed, a large number of women had consensual sexual relations, there was no bullying at PS 37 today, a lot of public officials did their job right, and most foreign nations were respectful of international treaties?

The same applies to our daily lives. If you are like most people, you are much more likely to gripe about your horrible morning commute than to rejoice in the fact that yesterday you had a smooth, carefree drive to work. When all that you remember at the end of the day is a list of things that went wrong today or annoying things that you have to do tomorrow, you will be stewing in negativity. But the truth is that on a daily basis most things that happen to you are not bad. Let's arbitrarily assume that by chance alone your experiences are 33 percent positive, 33 percent negative, and 33 percent neutral. When you are actively thinking only about the negative experiences, you are filling your brain 100 percent with negativity. What you need to do is actively start thinking about the positive experiences, to change that ratio.

Practicing gratitude means tracking the good things that happen.

Practicing gratitude is not just some vague, New Age overused practice that has no meaning behind it. Practicing gratitude is intended to shift your focus and give you a different perspective, by looking at the evidence more objectively. It is going to reverse the ratio of positive to neutral to negative events and will help you recalibrate your daily experiences. Practicing gratitude res̶e̶t̶s̶ the base rate. When the cloud of negativity makes for an overcast day, grab your journal and remind yourself of all the reasons you have to be celebrating your life. Doing so will keep you optimistic and energetic, and in action mode.

a. **Keep a journal.** Start by making a list at the end of the day of things that you enjoyed or you felt good about. Do it regularly. Be specific. You could include simple things, like I read a good book, I took a fun trip, or I ate a juicy orange. And also add weightier things, like profound insights that you had about yourself, exciting ideas you want to explore, or intense feelings that you experienced.

b. **Spotlight on excitement.** Make a pact with someone close to you and every six months ask each other these two questions:
- *What is the most exciting thing that happened to you in the last six months?*
- *What are you looking forward to in the next six months?*

Sharing exciting moments with someone else will make for a much more interesting dinner conversation than complaining about how busy you have been at work, how much you hate your bosses, and how dreadful the rat race is.

STRATEGY 2: FIND THE GEM

I have a close friend, whom I call the queen of exceptions. Whenever I make a negative statement about myself, someone else, or life in general, she always comes up with an exception. If I say I can't cook for the life of me, she remembers the one time when I made a delicious dish. If I say that this person is boring, she tells me she recently had an interesting conversation with him. She always finds facts that don't match my theory. And she can always find something positive to point out. At first, I was worried that she was just being oppositional, too kind, or too easy in her judgments. But then I realized that she has the amazing ability to find the gems in a boxful of pebbles.

Negativity makes you judgmental. And while you think you are being an astute observer, you are being biased, unfair, and hurtful. To break out of that habit of judging and criticizing, give yourself the following challenge:

As soon as you catch yourself thinking or talking negatively about someone or something, stop. Instead of letting the negative comments linger, actively search in your memory for something positive about the same person. Make it your mission to find the gem. Start challenging your negative opinions with opposite facts. If your judgment is about a person, think of something nice about them, something that you like or admire, or even something that you are jealous of. If your judgment is about a situation, think of its positive aspects or things you can learn from it, if only to be able to avoid it next time.

In fact, get in the habit of finding the gem even when

you are not thinking negatively about someone or something. Always aim to find one thing that you like.

Next time you are with someone and your judgments start creeping up, find the gem and share it with them. It could be something nice about what they are wearing, about what they just said, about the work they are doing, anything that would make them feel good to hear. But make sure it is a genuine comment. Not only are you defeating your negativity that way but you are also offering someone else a gift.

STRATEGY 3: NOTHING TO SAY? SAY NOTHING

Negativity will stop when you stop speaking negatively. If you find nothing positive or productive or helpful to say in a given situation, say nothing. Sometimes it is better not to say anything, to leave negative opinions unexpressed, and to let some things go without commentary, instead of judging, whining, or catastrophizing. If there is no good reason to gripe aimlessly, and there rarely is, protect yourself and others from the negative spin or the bad taste that your negative comments can create.

a. **Examine your intentions.** Before you say something negative, search for the reasons you want to say it. Is it because you are looking for sympathy? Do you want others to feel your pain? Or is it because you want to offer sympathy? Is it because you want to protect people from their own shortcomings? Or is it out of pure habit?

b. **Consider the effects.** Ask yourself, What purpose does this comment serve? How is it going to be helpful to you or to anyone else? Is it going to move you forward? Will it help you achieve your goal? Is it consistent with the kind of person you would like to become? Are you giving deliberate and constructive feedback? Are you describing a gem?

If you can't find a good answer to those questions, then say nothing.

STRATEGY 4: CLEAN UP YOUR SELF-TALK

If you insist on saying something, make sure you craft your message carefully. And start with your own self-talk.

Language is very powerful. It has the potential to shape your thinking and build your personality. Your self-talk is directly related to the visions you create, the goals you set, and the actions you take. This internal dialogue can move you leaps and bounds or stall you in the mire forever. Negative self-talk lurks quietly in your thoughts and affects how you feel and what you do.

To defeat negativity, start by changing negative self-talk. Speak to yourself in ways that support your actions and help you move forward with your goals. Speak of others in ways that can be a resource and inspiration to them. There are four steps to changing your self-talk from negative to productive:

STEP 1. Be curious. Your negative statements may sound like absolute truths or well-deliberated verdicts to you, but always allow for the possibility that your reasoning may have glitches. Be curious about your own conclusions and theories. Write them down, read them, and ask yourself: Why do I believe that? How did I draw this conclusion? Why do I think this way about this person? What makes me annoyed right now?

STEP 2. Speak to the facts. Many of the things you tell yourself are your own assumptions. They are things that you believe to be true without necessarily having proof. They are expressions of your attachment to your theories and effects of the glitches in reasoning.

How do you speak to the facts? You need to separate the facts from your assumptions. A few days ago, one of my clients barged into my office and said: I am angry, sad, and disappointed! Excellent, I said. Tell me why.* He told me that he was expecting a call from someone who never called him back. He used names to describe the other person that are very inappropriate to repeat and also said he felt completely irrelevant and neglected. After letting him vent for a little, I asked him to separate facts from assumptions. The facts were these: I called her. I left her a message. She hasn't called me back. The assumptions were these: She is unprofessional. She

---

* I do say that to my clients. Not because I am a sadist who likes it when people struggle with intense negative emotions, but because it gives us opportunities to practice brain management in vivo.

doesn't care about me. I am unimportant. I can't make it without her help. I wrote the statements down, in two different columns. He looked at them, thought it through, and said: "I am no longer angry and disappointed. She must have her own reasons for not calling back. I know I can still work on this project without her. But I am still sad that we may not get to work together." Fair enough.

So, if you want to speak to the facts, next time someone asks you whether the glass is half full or half empty a good answer is *it depends*. And a better answer is *the glass contains exactly 4.3 ounces of water.*

STEP 3. Avoid "big" words. Big words are absolutes—words that determine the size, the extent, and the importance of your theories. Absolutes polarize your thinking, leave you no options, distort the base rate, hide the evidence, maximize the consequences, and minimize the benefits. What are these big words? *Always, never, forever, each time, not once, the entire time, everyone, everybody, the whole world, nobody, none, everything, all of it, nothing, nil, zero, everywhere, nowhere, hate, love, best, worst, disaster, miracle.*

There is also a curious little word that very innocently tends to slip into language and take away the importance of something, leaving a very subtle negative taste: *just. Just* minimizes what follows as if it were unimportant or unworthy of praise, gratitude, or pride. *I just did what I had to. It was just a little help. It's just a college degree, no biggie. It's just a small business I run. I'm just another single mom.*

STEP 4. Form action questions. Whenever you catch yourself making a negative statement, turn it into an action question. See the statements in the chart below. The ones in the left column are typical of negative self-talk. The ones in the right column are action questions.

NEGATIVE STATEMENT	ACTION QUESTION
Replace ...	With ...
I can't do this	How can I do this?
There is nothing I can do	What can I do about it?
I don't know how to do this	How can I learn how to get it done?
No one can help	Who can I ask for help?
This is a huge problem	What are the potential solutions?
This is impossible!	What are the odds?
You are wrong!	What do you see that I don't?

If you are holding a glass and you can't decide if it is half full or half empty, ask yourself, What can I do with this amount of water? Questions beg for answers. Answers need action. Action leads to outcomes. Negativity stops you from asking questions. If there is no question, there is no search for the answer, no solution to the problem, and no success in achieving the goal.

STRATEGY 5: SNAP YOURSELF

One of the most basic concepts in psychology is that of reinforcement and punishment. Reinforcement is the attempt to increase the frequency of a behavior, while punishment is the attempt to decrease the frequency of a behavior. The term *negative reinforcement* is not the same as punishment. Negative reinforcement is actually what you do to stop something that feels like punishment. For example, when my stress levels get very high, I have to stop what I'm doing and go for a walk in the park. When I walk in the park, my anxiety goes down, I feel a lot calmer, and when I get back to what I was doing, I will be more creative and productive. Going for a walk in the park is negative reinforcement. Punishment, on the other hand, is what I do to stop me from doing something. Let's say that when I walk in the park, I also buy ice cream. We all know the effects of ice cream on our waists, so I need to find a way to stop eating ice cream when I go for a walk. To stop me from doing that, I pick an ice cream flavor that I don't like at all. Time after time, I will stop buying ice cream during my walks because now it feels more like punishment than pleasure.

A tiny amount of punishment can help you get rid of a large amount of negativity. The simplest form of punishment is to be subjected to something unpleasant as soon as you engage in the behavior you want to reduce. The punishment could involve applying a little pain (that was the idea behind spanking rambunctious children), taking away something (being grounded is a good example), or causing the body discomfort (taking medicine that makes you sick when you smoke a cigarette).

I went to a small business conference once, and at some point the organizers handed out a rubber band to each of us to put on our wrist. They told us that each time we had an unproductive thought about the growth potential of our business, we were to snap ourselves on the wrist with the rubber band. I thought this was a joke. I am a smart person with a PhD, and I know the theories behind these techniques well. Did they think that a little rubber band was going to work on me? (A great example of negativity. I should have immediately snapped myself.) I swallowed my pride and tried it. I was amazed at the results. First, it made me realize how often I was being negative. I had to constantly keep snapping. My wrist was red for days. And most important, the sting on my wrist made me want to change what I say to myself to avoid more self-punishment!

Do you want to see how negative you can be? Get yourself a rubber band and each time you say or think something negative, snap yourself. Do you make negative predictions about your future? Do you complain about your job? Do you put yourself or others down? Snap yourself! And don't go easy! You will see results pretty fast.

STRATEGY 6: AVOID THE BLACK HOLES

Negative people are like black holes. Like powerful magnets they pull everything in their orbits into their vortex

of despair. Even if you are not a negative person by dispo-
sition, it is very easy to be sucked into someone else's negativity. Being around people who constantly complain,
judge, and catastrophize can easily cast the shadow of
negativity on your own existence. Hearing about problems, failures, pain, trouble, distress, stalemates, obstacles, regrets, and gripes fills your mind with negative
images. Motivation and energy levels plummet, and fear
and worry grow. You may start questioning the chances
of your own success, the viability of your goals, the availability of opportunities, and the realism of your dreams.

You will be much more helpful to others, even a black
hole, when you can shine your bright light of optimism
and positivity on their darkness than by joining them in
their murky pit.

a. **Empathize, but don't identify.** You can be a good
   friend, a sympathetic ear, and a strong shoulder to
   cry on. Black holes need validation too! Express your
   sympathy, but remind yourself that this is their world
   and it doesn't have to be your world.

b. **Acknowledge, but don't accept.** Just like you, black
   holes have theories about the world, which they are
   willing to share and even impose. You can acknowledge their opinions, but you do not have to agree with
   them, and you definitely don't have to dismantle your
   own theory because they think theirs is better.

c. **Present the facts, but don't debate.** Focus on the
   facts and let them be heard. Don't try to persuade the

black holes that you are right and they are wrong. You will not go very far. Besides, your goal is to protect yourself from them, not to change them.

d. **Steer the conversation.** If you are entangled in a conversation with a black hole and you are starting to feel negativity's pull, take charge. Change the topic, ask neutral questions, or use the two questions from Strategy 1 on page 213.

Don't let yourself be swayed and don't feel obliged to stick around. When you find your judgment clouded, your energy dwindling, and your mood heading for the dumps, politely walk away.

STRATEGY 7: FIND THE FOUNTAINS OF POSITIVITY

The ultimate antidote to negativity is a strong injection of positivity. And the best source is another person with a rich supply of positivity. The same way that proximity to a black hole of negativity can drain you and leave you parched, surrounding yourself with positive, energetic, and supportive people can lift you up and spur you into action.

Positive people will encourage you to pursue your dreams, they will ask you questions that will help you see things from a different perspective, and they will boost your confidence. Interaction with a positive person will leave you more motivated, more inspired, and more energetic.

STEP 1. Identify people in your life who fit the profile. Fountains of positivity are the people whose words inspire you, whose work you admire, who make you feel good about yourself, who make you feel more energetic, who are listening to you with curiosity and excitement, who encourage you to keep working on your goals.

STEP 2. Make your list of five. These could be people you know personally or people you know through the press, conventional media, or social media.

STEP 3. Start connecting regularly. Meet up with them, invite them over for dinner, set up regular check-in phone calls. If they are people you don't know personally, find other ways to stay connected. Follow their blogs, read their books, watch their videos, attend their seminars.

Connect with these people not only when you feel like you are sliding down the slope of negativity but as often as you can. There is really no limit to how much good energy you can share with each other. Not to mention, there is no severe punishment for practicing positivity daily!

ONE LINK AT A TIME

Winston Churchill said: "It is a mistake to look too far ahead. Only one link of the chain of destiny can be handled at a time." The same rule applies to the actions that we take on a daily basis, actions that serve small and large goals alike. Reaching your goals will happen one action at a time.

I never told you how Peter went from quitting his job and being unemployed to becoming VP of sales for a multinational luxury brand. If you remember, Peter left his position as regional manager soon after an embarrassing moment during a meeting left him traumatized and paralyzed. His failure to deliver a presentation became synonymous with failure to perform his job duties. After he got a new job, things got worse. Plagued by self-doubt for months and terrified about ever being in the same situation again, he realized he needed to face his fears. He needed to be confronted with a threat, let his 4F (freeze, fight, flight, or fright) system go on full throttle, and learn how to harness it in the middle of the battle. And he started at the top of the list. He was going to challenge the fear of death. Peter decided to put himself in what he thought was a risky life-or-death situation, during which if he froze and hesitated to take action the cost could be enormous: He went zip-lining.

Fear of heights was included in his list of fears alongside public speaking, and zip-lining was the perfect opportunity to conquer the deepest of fears. Suspended over unknown territory, restrained only by the uncomfortable harness, with his feet dangling and his heart pounding, Peter knew that his only option after the trolley was released from the base would be to let gravity move him forward. When his feet touched the mat at the termination point, he knew he had won a crucial battle.

This was not the only thing that helped Peter get back on track. It was just the big jolt that he needed to unblock his brain from the shackles of self-doubt. To make that happen, he and I came up with a long-term plan. He knew that building confidence would require learning and practicing. He signed up for training courses in public speaking. He began practicing more. We used a scaffolding approach. He started by leading staff meetings first, and speaking at small events with only a handful of people. After each occasion, there was self-evaluation and feedback on his performance. This was followed by events a little larger in scope and numbers. Managing the brainblock was not always easy. Glitches continued to happen. About a year after he was hired, Peter applied for a higher position within the company. During a first interview with a human resources executive, he had a déjà vu of his experience from a couple of years earlier, when he was standing at the podium unable to utter anything comprehensible to his managers. Peter was brainblocked again. He knew that this interview wasn't the best sample of his performance. But this time he didn't lose his words. He composed himself, assumed his power pose, and was able to have a conversation with the interviewer, without running out of the room.

Eventually, he got the job.

THREE FINAL TIPS

Where there is a brain there will be a brainblock. Brain-blocks are subtle, they are hidden, and they are part of our machinery. Sometimes they appear as moments of weakness and momentary lapses, and other times as deeply rooted character traits. All they are is misplaced effort, misguided action that interferes with the pursuit of a goal. And the goal of brain management is not to eliminate the brainblocks, but to redirect the action.

1. Instead of thinking about how to get rid of brain-blocks, which is a prevention goal and may get you entangled in perfectionism, think about how to im-prove your skills:

   - *How to manage fear better.*
   - *How to get started when you're stuck.*

- *How to be more patient and serene.*
- *How to harness your attention.*
- *How to be more open and creative.*
- *How to prioritize what's important.*
- *How to make better decisions and enjoy life more.*

2. There are forty-nine strategies available to you in this book, and some of them have several substrategies. While the number of strategies may be too large to remember and you may find it difficult to apply all of them, as a group these strategies provide you with a wide range of options. Some of them will be more appealing and more suitable to you. After you read them all:
   - *Pick your* three *favorite strategies to master.*
   - *Memorize them.*
   - *Apply them as often as you can.*

3. If there were only one message to share in this book, it would be the following:

   Always
   - **Know your goal.** *Be aware of your intentions. We live 90 percent of our lives on automatic pilot. Make sure you live the other 10 percent fully conscious.*
   - **Know what you need to do.** *Be aware of the actions you need to take to achieve that goal. The less you know about how to make something happen, the less likely that it will happen.*
   - **Know what you are doing.** *Be aware of your action*

in the moment. Monitor yourself to make sure your actions are aligned with your goals.

- ***Know your brainblocks.*** *Be aware of the signs and symptoms. When you notice something, call it out. That is the first and most important step of brain management.*

On that note, let me stop before the brainblock of perfectionism takes over!

Enjoy your journey from dreamer to achiever.

ACKNOWLEDGMENTS

Writing this book wouldn't be possible without the input, the wisdom, and the support of so many people.

THE PROFESSIONALS

My deepest appreciation to my editor Jeanette Shaw for her incisive feedback, her skillful chiseling of the text, her patience with my unfamiliarity, and her kind encouragement.

My gratitude to my agent, Jeff Herman, who extended me his trust and guided me through the gates of the publishing world.

Many thanks to Marian Lizzi, Lauren Becker, John Duff, and the team at Prentice Hall Press for their invaluable help in bringing the book to life. A big thank-you to Eric Fuentecilla, the cover designer who translated my words into the most beautiful visual concept I could ask for.

THE LOVED ONES

I can't thank the people in my life enough for being a source of inspiration, love, and support during all the stages of development of the book. Without their continuous encouragement and feedback, this book would have remained another New Year's resolution that got stuck in a drawer.

To my family—my mother, Despina, and my brother, George—for their unconditional love and endless support.

To Andre, for being the most wonderful partner during this process. Who stood by my side silently and took on all the responsibilities that I had neglected while writing the book.

To my friends, Luba Roytburd, for her loyalty and support and for being the embodiment of perseverance; Kari Taylor-Evans, for our inspiring peer consultations while running in Central Park; Dimitra Trypani, for her perennial support and her unsolicited preproduction promotion; Sophia Hatzivassiliou, for putting up with my endless brainstorming monologues and helping me stay focused; Chris Rentis, for forgiving me for spending half of our time together working on the book; George Georgiadis, for being my muse; Kostas Karathanos, Brooke Wilson, Yianis Sarafidis, and Lisa Bryant for believing in my cause.

THE TEACHERS

From the bottom of my heart and the depths of my brain, I would like to extend my gratitude to my colleagues and supervisors, who have taught me everything I know about the brain, its functions and dysfunctions, and how to best help the people who I work with: Dr. Len Travaglione, Dr. Teresa Ashman, Dr. Wayne Gordon, and Dr. Dave Layman. A special thanks to the late Dr. Joshua Cantor, who was able to find the gem in every person he met.

THE CLIENTS

Without the trust, courage, and openness my clients have shown over the years, my understanding of what works and what doesn't would be restricted, my vision limited, and my mission aborted. Writing this book would not be possible without their invaluable input.

THE STRANGERS

A big thank-you to the staff at United Airlines for many uninterrupted flight hours of writing. To the staff at the Starbucks, the Koffeecake Corner, and Pier i Café, for letting me use their facilities and free Wi-Fi for many hours of continuous writing.

NOTES

■ ■ ■ ■ ■ ■ ■

INTRODUCTION

1   "New Year's Resolution Statistics," Statistic Brain, statistic brain.com/new-years-resolution-statistics.

BRAINBLOCK #1

1   S. H. Bracha, "Freeze, Flight, Fight, Fright, Faint: Adaptionist Perspectives on the Acute Stress Response Spectrum," *CNS Spectrums* 9 (2004): 679–85.

2   K. Albrecht, "The (Only) Five Fears We All Share," *Psychology Today*, March 22, 2012, psychologytoday.com/blog/brainsnacks/201203/the-only-5-fears-we-all-share.

3   M. Gladwell, *Outliers: The Story of Success* (New York: Little, Brown, 2008).

4   A. Cuddy, "Your Body Language Shapes Who You Are," filmed June 2012, ted.com/talks/amy_cuddy_your_body_language_shapes_who_you_are.html.

BRAINBLOCK #2

1   T. A. Pychyl, M. M. Lee, R. Thibodeau, and A. Blunt, "Five Days of Emotion: An Experience Sampling Study of Undergraduate Student Procrastination," *Journal of Social Behavior and Personality* 15 (2000): 135–50.

2   D. C. Watson, "Procrastination and the Five-Factor Model: A Facet Level Analysis," *Personality and Individual Differences* 30 (2001): 149–58.

3   J. L. Cummings and B. L. Miller, "Conceptual and Clinical Aspects of the Frontal Lobes," in *The Human Frontal Lobes*, 2nd ed., ed. B. L. Miller and J. L. Cummings (New York: Guilford Press, 2007), 12–21.

4   L. A. Rabin, J. Fogel, and K. E. Nutter-Upham, "Academic Procrastination in College Students: The Role of Self-Reported Executive Function," *Journal of Clinical and Experimental Neuropsychology* 33 (2011): 344–57.

5   Ibid.

BRAINBLOCK #3

1   J. Barling and R. Boswell, "Work Performance and the Achievement-Strivings and Impatience-Irritability Dimensions of Type A Behavior," *Applied Psychology: An International Review* 44 (1995): 143–53.

2   R. Gomez, "Impatience-Aggression, Competitiveness, and Avoidant Coping: Direct and Moderating Effects on Maladjustment Among Adolescents," *Personality and Individual Differences* 25 (1998): 649–61.

3   "Stress: The Different Kinds of Stress," American Psychological Association, apa.org/helpcenter/stress-kinds.aspx.

4   M. Davis, E. R. Eshelman, and M. McKay, *The Relaxation and Stress Reduction Workbook* (Oakland, CA: New Harbinger Publications, 1995).

BRAINBLOCK #4

1   D. L. Strayer, F. A. Drews, and D. J. Crouch, "A Comparison of the Cell Phone Driver and the Drunk Driver," *Human Factors* 48 (2006): 381–91.

2   M. M. Sohlberg and C. A. Mateer, *A Direct Attention Training Program for Persons with Acquired Brain Injury* (Wake Forest, NC: Lash & Associates, 2011).

3   Paolo, Cardini, "Forget Multitasking, Try Monotasking," filmed June 2012, ted.com/talks/paolo_cardini_forget_multitasking_try_monotasking.html.

BRAINBLOCK #5

1   M. Becker, "Einstein on Misattribution: 'I Probably Didn't Say That,'" *Becker's Online Journal*, November 13, 2012, news.hypercrit.net/2012/11/13/einstein-on-misattribution-i-probably-didnt-say-that.

2   B. Rende, "Cognitive Flexibility: Theory, Assessment, and

Treatment," *Seminars in Speech and Language* 21 (2000): 121–33.

3   J. Haden, "9 People You Must Remove from Your Inner Circle," *Inc.*, last updated October 15, 2012, inc.com/jeff-haden/9-people-you-must-remove-from-your-inner-circle.html.

BRAINBLOCK #6

1   J. Stoeber and S. Hotham, "Perfectionism and Social Desirability: Students Report Increased Perfectionism to Create a Positive Impression," *Personality and Individual Differences* 55 (2013): 626–29.

2   A. J. Bergman, J. E. Nyland, and L. R. Burns, "Correlates with Perfectionism Using a Dual Process Model," *Personality and Individual Differences* 43 (2007): 389–99.

3   P. D. Slade, D. B. Coppel, and B. D. Townes, "Neurocognitive Correlates of Positive and Negative Perfectionism," *International Journal of Neuroscience* 119 (2009): 1741–54.

4   A. A. Scholer and E. T. Higgins, "Promotion and Prevention Systems: Regulatory Focus Dynamics Within Self-Regulatory Hierarchies," in *Handbook of Self Regulation*, 2nd ed., ed. K. D. Vohs and R. F. Baumeister (New York: Guilford Press, 2011), 143–61.

5   C. S. Carver and M. F. Scheier, "Self-Regulation of Action and Affect," in *Handbook of Self Regulation*, 2nd ed., ed. K. D. Vohs and R. F. Baumeister (New York: Guilford Press, 2011), 3–21.

6   R. Pierson, "Every Kid Needs a Champion," filmed May 2013, ted.com/talks/rita_pierson_every_kid_needs_a_champion.

7   Apple Press Info, apple.com/pr/products/ipodhistory.

BRAINBLOCK #7

1   The original study by I. E. Dror, D. Charlton, and A. Peron (2006) was cited in J. Kukucka and S. M. Kassin, "Do Confessions Taint Perceptions of Handwriting Evidence? An Empirical Test of Forensic Confirmation Bias," *Law and Human Behavior* 38 (2014): 256–70.

2   E. J. Fox, "Number of U.S. Millionaires Hits New High," CNN

Money, March 14, 2014, money.cnn.com/2014/03/14/news/economy/us-millionaires-households.

3 P. N. Murray, "Inside the Consumer Mind," *Psychology Today*, February 26, 2013, psychologytoday.com/blog/inside-the-consumer-mind/201302/how-emotions-influence-what-we-buy.

INDEX

∎ ∎ ∎ ∎ ∎ ∎

Page numbers in **bold** indicate tables; those followed by "n" indicate notes.